In the Countryside
Moss Taylor

wren
publishing

By the same author
The Birds of Sheringham
The Birds of Norfolk (co-author)
Guardian Spirit of the East Bank

First published 2003
Copyright © Moss Taylor
Wren Publishing, 4 Heath Road, Sheringham, Norfolk, NR26 8JH

Design by Nik Taylor
Front cover by Robert Gillmor

ISBN 0-9542545-1-1

Printed in Great Britain by Crowes Complete Print, Norwich, Norfolk.

Contents

As autumn leaves fall

In the bleak midwinter

Introduction

In July 1999, I was invited to join Percy Trett, Rex Hancy and Grace Corne as one of the Eastern Daily Press "In the Countryside" columnists. This followed the untimely death of Michael Seago, who had been one of the team for many years. At the time, I considered it a great honour, and still do, to have been asked to follow in the footsteps of such illustrious local naturalists as Arthur Patterson, Ted Ellis, Michael Seago and the other members of the current team.

The frequent letters, phone calls and emails that I receive from EDP readers leads me to hope that this publication of a selection of my columns will be welcomed. All those reproduced in this book appeared in the EDP between August 1999 and December 2001. They are largely unchanged apart from a few minor alterations to one or two of the texts. All of the colour photographs were taken by me on field trips in East Anglia or on my travels abroad.

The highly evocative and attractive front cover is from a three-colour linocut print designed by Robert Gillmor. I feel privileged that such a fine artist should have agreed to undertake this commission for which I thank him most sincerely.

During my four years as an EDP columnist, I have received great assistance and encouragement from my sub-editors, Ian Bullock and, more recently, Pete Kelly. I am most grateful to both of them. I would also like to acknowledge the help given by Mike Dawson at the printers, Crowes Complete Print of Norwich, and the patience shown, yet again, by my son Nik, during the design stages. If this small book encourages readers to be more aware of, and appreciate, the wonders in the countryside, then I shall be more than happy.

Moss Taylor

Springtime is here

Delighted to hear the song of a "fulfer"

February 2000
While walking across the parkland at Felbrigg last week, I was delighted to hear the strident song of a mistle thrush, despite the day being overcast and very windy. This habit of singing in stormy weather, often from the most exposed and highest branches of a tall tree, has resulted in the bird being known as "storm-cock", although in Norfolk its vernacular name is "fulfer".

The name mistle thrush, in fact, is derived from the specific part of its Latin name of *viscivorus*, which translated literally means mistletoe devourer. In Britain, however, this particular fruit does not form a major part of its diet, where its favourite berries are holly and yew. Mistle thrushes are often very vigorous in their defence of a holly tree during the winter months, at least until the berry crop has been fully devoured.

Mistle thrushes are also one of the earliest species to nest in the spring, usually building in a fork of a large tree, and often having eggs by the end of February or early March. Interestingly these early nests are often more successful than the later ones, probably because predators such as jays and grey squirrels are not actively looking for nests this early in the season.

To me, mistle thrushes epitomise parkland, along with such species as jackdaws, stock doves, little owls and Egyptian geese. As with much of today's landscape, parkland is a man-made habitat, often the relic of a mediaeval deer park. Typically, it consists of widely scattered ancient trees, often with much dead and dying timber, set in open grassland.

Apart from the mistle thrush, most of the breeding birds in parkland are hole nesters, even the rather gawky Egyptian geese. Introduced from Africa in the eighteenth century, to adorn "gentlemen's ponds", they have never really achieved their true potential and have remained largely confined to East Anglia. This is partly due to their habit of nesting in the early part of the year, when many of the young perish in adverse weather. Their raucous calls can often be located to the lower branches of a parkland tree where the birds sit near their nesting holes.

But perhaps the most typical parkland birds are the jackdaws. They are extremely sociable birds, which often nest in loose colonies in trees, several pairs not infrequently occupying different holes in the same trunk. They are almost invariably seen together in pairs, just watch a party of them flying around above you, to confirm this interesting fact for yourself.

Getting ready for summer plumage

March 2000

During the course of the next few weeks, many of our birds will begin to assume the brighter colours of their breeding plumage. For many species, this only involves the males, as the females will need to remain relatively dull, in order to avoid detection while at the nest, especially during incubation of the eggs. However, for hole-nesting birds, such as the nuthatch, woodpeckers and tits, this sexual dimorphism, as it is called, is not necessary as the female remains well concealed in the nesting cavity.

But how do birds achieve this change from winter to summer plumage? For the majority of passerines, or small perching birds, it is simply a matter of the feather tips wearing away as winter progresses, to expose the more intense colours further down the shaft, often involving primarily the head.

Take for example starlings. During winter, their plumage is characterised by extensive white or pale spotting, especially on the underparts. As the white feather tips wear away, the glossy, iridescence of their breeding dress is gradually revealed. The same process is responsible for the appearance in spring of the blue crown of the chaffinch and the uniformly black head and orange breast of the male brambling, which makes it such a striking bird in spring.

For other groups of birds, such as the waders, breeding plumage is achieved as a direct result of a late winter body moult. Many species of wader have white underparts during the winter, moulting to black or red for the summer. For instance grey and golden plovers have extensive black breasts and bellies in breeding plumage, while knots and bar-tailed godwits show rich chestnut underparts.

But perhaps the most marked changes occur in male ruffs, which in addition grow the neck ruff that can vary in colour from white, through brown to black. These of course are best seen when the males perform their elaborate communal displays at the leks.

Like the finches, buntings also attain their breeding plumage by feather tip wear during the course of the winter and early spring. Possibly the most attractive bunting that I have ever seen was the fine male Siberian meadow bunting, which was present in the sand dunes below the L'Estrange Hotel at Hunstanton in February. Although considered to be an escaped cage bird, it was well worth the trip to see such a beautifully marked bird, with its bold black and white head pattern set off by warm chestnut ear coverts.

It's always worth checking gulls

March 2001

On occasions, the most unlikely of days turn out to be the most interesting, as happened to me only a couple of weeks ago. The events also brought home to me the importance of checking out carefully every bird that one sees. A maxim that I was taught on one of my very first visits to Cley, almost 40 years ago.

After a grey and rather misty start to the day, a weak sun had begun to filter through the clouds as I drove along the coast road to Weybourne. A stream of black-headed gulls were following the plough, while nearby a couple of hundred more were resting and preening, having satiated their appetites on the worms and other grubs that had been brought to the surface earlier in the day. Something made me stop and check them out, and while going through the flock of resting birds I came to a much smaller gull, with some black on the crown and a dark bar across the closed wing - a first-winter little gull. Not a species that I normally associate with ploughing operations. The stop had been worthwhile.

After parking in Lower Kelling village, I took the track that leads past the Quags, where there was the usual selection of wintering wildfowl, but again I decided to check them all out individually. Four teal in a small pool particularly caught my attention, one of them looked odd, but what was it that seemed strange? Then I realised. One had the chestnut and green head markings of a drake but the mottled, brown body of a female. As drake teal normally develop their adult plumage during their first winter, I can only assume that this bird had only partially-moulted, but it certainly presented a very unusual appearance.

Further along the track, near the village of Salthouse, a family party of mute swans fed in a dyke, and again for no obvious reason I decided to check them with binoculars. Exactly why I did was a mystery, but I could scarcely believe my eyes when I realised that one of the younger birds was in fact a first-winter whooper swan, paler and greyer than the young mutes and with the distinctive bill pattern apparent, although it was not yet showing any yellow.

Returning along the shingle bank, a scan through another group of black-headed gulls produced a fine adult Mediterranean gull, complete with black hood; while the seventh gull species of the morning, a lesser black-backed, on Kelling Water Meadows, was an indication that spring passage was underway.

The first wheatear - a moment to savour

March 2000

The middle of March is the time that we can start looking and listening out for the first returning summer migrants, after their long journeys from southern Europe or North Africa. For many birdwatchers, myself included, the sighting of the first wheatear of the spring is a moment to be savoured. For me it usually involves a handsome cock bird (Plate 2), unmistakable with his blue-grey back, black mask and warm buff flush on the breast, either flitting along behind the shingle bank at Weybourne or on the cliff-top path at Sheringham. Wherever it is, that first flash of its white rump is pure joy. Spring has at last arrived - or more often than not, is just a few weeks away!!

At about the same time, the first Sandwich terns of the spring are often recorded offshore. They are the largest of the terns which breed in Norfolk, with dazzling white upperparts, the black crown adorned with a shaggy crest and the long black bill has a yellow tip.

Of the hirundines (members of the swallow family), the sand martin is usually the first seen in the spring, with the earliest often recorded along the coast by mid-March. Unlike the swallow, its upperparts are grey-brown and it has a brown breast band across its whitish underparts.

In the woods, this is the time to listen out for the first chiffchaffs of the spring. Like the first wheatear, the first singing chiffchaff is a sound that never fails to thrill. Its song is one of the easiest to remember, "chiff-chaff, chiff-chaff, chiff-chiff-chaff", or a simple variation on this theme. To the beginner, however, a coal tit's song is not dissimilar and always beware of the amazing mimicry shown by some great tits!

But perhaps the most controversial first spring arrival dates are for cuckoos, as is apparent by the number of reader's letters published recently in the EDP! While wishing to remain impartial, I would like to make two points. Firstly, the earliest ever, fully authenticated cuckoos in Norfolk were both in 1903, at Horsey on March 21 and at Yarmouth eight days later (and this was 50 years before the first collared dove appeared in Britain!). In fact, there have only been two other March records in Norfolk, at Blakeney and Surlingham both on March 29, 1965. Secondly, early cuckoos tend to be recorded in years in which other spring migrants arrive early, and this year both wheatear and house martin were seen before the end of February!

Brimstone butterfly's gunpowder connections

March 2000

As the days lengthen and temperatures begin to rise, we can look forward to seeing the first butterflies on the wing. In the same way that I look forward with keen anticipation to the first wheatear of the spring, the first sighting of a brimstone is another sign that winter really is over.

Brimstones overwinter as adult butterflies, often in clumps of ivy, but their pale greenish underwings and leaf-shaped outline make them extremely difficult to locate. For this reason, winter survival may be as high as 85%. The brighter yellow males emerge first, thus making it more likely that they will be able to locate unmated females by the time that they first appear, two or three weeks later.

Brimstones feed on the nectar of primroses, of which they are an important pollinator; their long tongues enabling them to reach the nectar from inside the deep flowers. They are common butterflies throughout southern England, being seen along woodland edges, thickets and hedgerows.

Having mated, the females search out purging and alder buckthorn on which to lay their eggs, the two food plants of the brimstone caterpillars. Like the adults, the larvae are well camouflaged and often rest along the midribs of the leaves. Interestingly, both sexes appear together in July after pupation, as they will not be pairing until the following spring and their only aim then is to feed up prior to hibernation. They are long-lived butterflies, some adults surviving from the time they appear in July through to the following June.

I am always fascinated by the origin of species' names. The word "butterfly" probably refers to the yellow colour of the brimstone, while the name "brimstone" is an allusion to the yellow colour of sulphur.

The bark and berries of one of its food plants, the purging buckthorn, were extensively used in former times as a purgative. However, following the discovery of the milder effects of cascara, which is obtained from a related North American shrub, its use declined! Its other food plant, the alder buckthorn, has also been used by man in a surprising number of ways - as a laxative, a dye and for meat skewers. But perhaps the most interesting was its use in producing high-quality charcoal, used in the production of gunpowder.

Of gunpowder's three ingredients - charcoal and sulphur are both associated with the brimstone, I wonder if anyone can find a connection with the third ingredient - saltpetre?

Dartford warblers are back in Suffolk

September 2000
The announcement by the RSPB, that the Dartford warbler is now firmly established as a breeding bird on the coastal heaths of Suffolk, is excellent news. They are closely related to whitethroats, the more familiar and widespread summer visitors to our hedgerows.

If seen well, Dartford warblers are unmistakable with their blue-grey upperparts, wine-red underparts and long, cocked-up tail. Unfortunately, however, they spend much of their time creeping through the tangle of gorse and heather in which they live, only occasionally perching in full view on top of a bush.

From a single pair, which possibly bred on Dunwich Heath in 1995, the Suffolk population has now increased to 33 breeding pairs and nine additional singing males - and all this in only five years. The best sites at which to see these delightful birds are Dunwich Heath and the RSPB's Minsmere Reserve.

Unusually for a warbler, this species is resident in England, and therefore is particularly susceptible to runs of cold winters. Their return to Suffolk may be partly due to the recent mild winters, but whether they have recolonised from their British stronghold in southern England or from France is uncertain.

Although the species still remains a rarity in Norfolk, it may well follow the pattern shown in Suffolk. One reason why Dartford warblers have recolonised Suffolk is the good management of heathland there in recent years. The restoration of Norfolk heathland is also now a conservation priority being tackled by a group that includes Norfolk Wildlife Trust and English Nature.

In North Norfolk, traditional heathland management on Kelling and Salthouse Heaths was abandoned many years ago. Previously this would have involved grazing and the use of gorse as firewood. Since these were discontinued, the gorse has spread shading out much of the heather, while birches have invaded the area and if left unchecked would eventually result in it reverting to woodland. Although the gorse clearance and burning on Kelling and Salthouse Heaths last winter attracted some criticism, Dartford warblers may well colonise north Norfolk in the future as a direct result. This important work was only made possible by a substantial grant from the Heritage Lottery Fund.

Three other typical heathland birds, the nightjar, woodlark and stonechat will also benefit from this type of management. If nature had been allowed to take its course, the heaths would eventually have become dense, mixed deciduous woodland, and all the unique heathland wildlife would have disappeared.

Birdsong is a language with many dialects

May 2000

A few months ago my wife Fran happened to say to me "Isn't it interesting how all birds speak the same language?". What she meant, of course, was that all birds of the same species apparently have identical songs, whether they live in Britain, France or Germany, for instance.

If you can recognise the song of a chaffinch in England, then you should be able to pick out one singing on the Continent. However, while this is broadly true, the songs are actually subtly different, with birds in different areas singing in local dialects. Even within the same area, each male will have a slightly different song from his neighbour. Listen carefully to the yellowhammer's familiar "Little bit of bread and no cheese" and you will spot variations on the common theme.

The main purpose of birdsong is species recognition - it allows a female to recognise a male and indicates to any rival males the extent of the songster's territory. It has long been known that female birds are more attracted to males with more complicated and more sophisticated songs. The exact reasons for this have been debatable. However, new research indicates that males with more melodious songs also make more frequent visits to the nest to feed the young. These then grow more rapidly and presumably are healthier and stronger, and therefore more likely to survive. Thus it appears to be this association that attracts the female to a particular male.

I recently received a letter from EDP reader Mary Manning from Old Catton, asking about a blackbird which she heard singing "delicately and gently", last summer, in a beech hedge in her garden. This very subdued, quiet form of singing is called "subsong", and I have heard it on many occasions over the years, mainly from robins and the *Sylvia* warblers, such as blackcap and whitethroat.

In the autumn, subsong appears to be young birds practising for the following spring, and in fact trying to learn the "correct" song. It may well have the same purpose during the spring and summer, but also could simply be the bird playing around and just entertaining himself - rather like us humming a tune!

Another fascinating aspect of birdsong is the ability of many species to mimic. Perhaps the best-known of the common birds is the starling, which can have a very varied song. Recently on the BBC programme Look East, a tame, hand-reared one was featured from Northamptonshire that had a vocabulary of 30 words!

Farmland rooks are bucking the trend

April 2000

On a recent trip to Scotland, I was impressed by the number of rooks that we passed as we drove north from East Anglia to the Lowlands. Without doubt they were the commonest and most numerous species encountered. But why are the rooks prospering when so many of our other farmland birds are in serious decline?

As rooks feed almost exclusively on open areas of grassland and arable land, they were probably confined to the chalk downs of southern England before the Middle Ages. However, by Tudor times, as more woodland was cleared, they had become well established throughout the country.

Both in Norfolk and nationally, a decline in rook numbers was noted between 1946 and 1975, which was attributed to changes in agricultural practices such as a loss of grazing land, a change to autumn-sown cereals and perhaps the use of pesticides. But since 1980, despite the continuing and increasing intensification of agriculture, rooks have been able to buck the trend and have actually increased in numbers! A British Trust for Ornithology survey showed a total of 1.27 million rooks' nests in the United Kingdom in 1996, an increase of 39% since 1975.

Rooks are highly colonial, nesting in groups of only a handful to many hundreds, usually in tall deciduous or coniferous trees in small stands or lines, rather than in large woods. Like jackdaws, they remain in pairs throughout the year and by early spring nesting activity at a rookery is well under way. In fact the best time to count the number of nests is in March or early April, before bud burst conceals the location of the individual nests.

The sudden irruption of all the adults from a rookery creates a most impressive sight and sound. The causes of such "outflights" or "dreads" are varied and can be no more than rooks quarrelling within the colony, jackdaws or crows giving their warning calls, the sound of an aircraft or gunshot, or commonly human disturbance below the nests.

But returning to my original question, what factors have allowed the rook to increase in recent years? Is it related to the rapid spread of outdoor pig farms, or the ban on stubble burning or climatic change resulting in milder winters? Perhaps, it is simply that rooks are omnivorous and can adapt their diet to whatever is available. May be we should be putting more effort in to studying a species that is successful, rather than concentrating on those that are in decline?

Migrants from the moors and mountains

May 2000

One of my favourite spring passage birds is the ring ouzel. Its flighty nature and distinctive, metallic "tac, tac, tac" call, epitomise for me the wild and desolate moorlands and mountains of northern and western Britain, where it breeds. Unfortunately, however, its numbers have been declining for many years, even though it still remains a reasonably common spring migrant in Norfolk.

Despite its wariness, the male, at least, is easy to recognise, even if seen only briefly or at a distance. About the size of a blackbird but longer winged, the male is entirely black apart from a broad white crescent across the breast and pale edges to the flight feathers. The female is more similar to a female blackbird, but with scaly underparts and often only a suggestion of a pale buff breast band.

Those which breed in the British Isles and Scandinavia, winter in southern Europe and north-west Africa, and we see them in Norfolk as they make their way north in spring.

The earliest are usually reported in late March and passage continues into late May. While such sites as cliff-top fields, coastal golf courses and dunes are the most likely places to see them, increasing numbers have been located inland in Norfolk during the 1990s. I have certainly found that the grazing meadows around the lake at Felbrigg Park, in North Norfolk, invariably hold one or two each spring, often in the company of late redwings and fieldfares, with which they presumably migrate north back to their Scandinavian breeding grounds. Also this year, the Hangs at Cley have hosted parties of up to 10, which have proved very popular with both local and visiting birdwatchers alike.

Although ring ouzels have never bred in Norfolk, and given the East Anglian landscape, are never likely to do so, occasional birds linger for a few days in spring. I well remember a fine adult male that remained at Weybourne for almost a week last year. During its stay, it frequently sang from a low hillock, its song recalling that of a mistle thrush.

Like the mistle thrush, it also has an interesting collection of local names (but thankfully not in Norfolk - unless, of course, someone knows different!) most of which refer to its favoured summer haunts - thus "heath throstle", "mountain blackbird", "rock starling" and "tor ouzel", as well as "hill chack", from its call.

Why are male birds so brightly coloured?

April 2001
Now is the time of year, when we can fully appreciate the attractive plumage of many of our common birds. But why is it, that in many species, the males are more brightly coloured than the females?

Courtship plays an important role in ensuring that birds recognise others of the same species, find a member of the opposite sex and hopefully pair up and success-fully raise young. The brightly coloured feathers of male birds are often part of this courtship display, along with the individual songs that are unique to each species.

The greatest diversity of colour is often found amongst groups of birds, in which several similar species gather to display in the same general area. This is particularly well shown in the smaller wildfowl. One has only to look at the plumage patterns and distribution of colours in drakes, compared with the rather plain, mottled brown of most ducks, irrespective of species, to appreciate the great variety that exists. In fact, sorting out unaccompanied female ducks can be one of the most difficult identifi-cation problems. Clearly, the females are being attracted to drakes exhibiting specific colours and patterns, often around the head and neck, and shown to their best advantage by the exaggerated head movements used by many species.

In other birds, such as the great crested grebe, there is very little sexual dimor-phism, that is difference in the appearance of the two sexes. In this species, as must have been witnessed by many readers visiting the Broads, both birds take an equally active role when performing their highly ritualised displays. The commonest of which is the appropriately named "Head-shaking Ceremony", when the pair face each other with necks erect and shake their heads slowly from side to side.

In general, in species which construct open nests, the females are dull brown to avoid detection whilst incubating, such as is seen in the chaffinch and most species of duck. On the other hand, in hole-nesting birds, the females are often nearly as brightly coloured as the males, a good example being the blue tit. The same even holds true for the shelduck, which typically nests underground in a rabbit burrow.

But perhaps the most interesting examples of sexual dimorphism occur in the dotterel (Plate 2) and phalaropes, species of waders that demonstrate almost complete role reversal. The more brightly coloured females display to the duller plumaged males and once mating has occurred and the clutch has been completed, it is the males' responsibility to incubate the eggs and take care of the young, once hatched. Surely the founders of women's lib!

Bird that cheered war-weary Londoners

May 2001

This spring I've been fortunate enough to see four black redstarts. The first, in late March, was a most handsome adult male that graced the RAF buildings on the old camp at Weybourne. With its quivering, fiery-red tail and bold white wing patch contrasting with the rest of its sooty black plumage, it was a real joy to watch. But the fourth one, albeit a much duller female, was perhaps the most exciting, appearing, as it did, in my garden in early April. It fed briefly on the vegetable garden before moving on.

In the British Isles, the black redstart is very much an urban bird during the breeding season. It first began to breed regularly in the London area in 1926, with Inner London being colonised during the second world war. How their presence must have lifted the hearts of the war-weary Londoners. In fact, it was as a direct result of the many derelict bomb-sites, that numbers of black redstarts began to increase, as they utilised these otherwise unappealing areas, as breeding sites. As the bomb-sites were redeveloped, so the population began to decline.

Here in East Anglia, it has always been a scarce breeding bird, being confined mainly to the larger coastal towns. In Norfolk the species first bred in 1950, with two pairs in bombed buildings at Yarmouth and a third pair nesting in an air-raid shelter at Gorleston. Once again maintaining their links with wartime!

In 1973, Peter Allard, one of the co-authors of the recently published, Nature in East Norfolk, organised a survey of black redstarts in the Yarmouth area, and found a surprising total of 18 singing males, in and around buildings. Breeding was confirmed for 17 pairs and at least 50 young were successfully fledged. Since then, numbers have fallen to just a handful of pairs, but Yarmouth remains the stronghold within the county.

I well remember when I first moved to Sheringham in 1972, hearing one singing in the middle of town, although initially I couldn't locate the bird, nor could I recognise the song. They have a remarkable ability to sing from rooftops, but always just out of sight of the observer! It subsequently transpired that they were breeding in an old garage near the seafront, although the site was only used for two years. Several years later the old derelict huts on the RAF camp at Weybourne were used successfully by a pair for a number years, until they were all demolished in the early 1980s.

Exhilarating exaltation of skylarks

May 2000

Last week my wife and I spent a very enjoyable morning wandering through the dunes and along the beach at Winterton. For Fran, who was born and brought up in Gorleston, it was a return to her own part of Norfolk; while for me it brought back happy memories of one of my favourite birding areas, when I lived in Yarmouth in the late 1960s.

We had left Sheringham in glorious sunshine, with an unbroken blue sky, but unfortunately, the easterly breeze had produced one of those annoying sea frets, which rolled across the dunes like a fine mountain mist. Winterton Dunes National Nature Reserve extends to over a hundred hectares and apart from the sand dunes immediately behind the beach, consists largely of a coastal heath. The vegetation is dominated by heather, while lower cover is provided by sand sedge, which helps to bind together the dunes, clumps of sheep's fescue and a variety of lichens. All of which combine to produce a rich mosaic of greens.

We were soon surrounded by an exaltation of skylarks (surely one of the most appropriate collective nouns for birds?), pouring out their songs as they soared in the sky above us; while the scratchy song of a whitethroat could be heard coming from some nearby bushes. As on all "blasted" heaths, the vegetation tends to be short and this is well demonstrated at Winterton by the stunted birches and low-growing gorse bushes. The latter ablaze with bright yellow flowers, which filled the air with their delightful coconut-like aroma.

A handsome cock stonechat, with his black head, white half-collar and deep orange breast, perched atop one of the bushes and was soon joined by his more dowdy mate. From there the pair scalded us with their harsh alarm calls, sounding exactly like two stones being knocked together, from whence their name "stonechat" originates.

As we crossed towards the sea, three ring ouzels suddenly exploded from a dune slack and flew rapidly inland. Approaching the beach, we were greeted by the calls of little terns and a female ringed plover which started to perform her "broken wing" display. Looking as if she couldn't fly, she stumbled along the sand, rolling from side to side, helplessly flicking her wings. Once she had led us far enough away from her nest, she miraculously "recovered" and flew off strongly down to the water's edge! Let's hope that other walkers and their dogs are just as easily fooled!

Watch out for those later spring migrants

May 2001

By now many of our summer migrants will have completed their long and hazardous journey from their African wintering areas. It's strange how living on the coast, many species seem to slip in unnoticed. Although I've only recorded a few migrant willow warblers this spring, the woods inland of Sheringham are alive with their songs, as well as those of blackcaps and even a few garden warblers.

Several people have commented to me about the late arrival of swallows this spring and they did seem to be fairly scarce throughout April. The short spell of warmer weather at the end of the month, however, certainly saw an increase in numbers passing through East Anglia and hopefully most pairs will have returned to their barns in the next week or so. As with most summer migrants, it's the males that return first, to reclaim their territories from the previous year. Ringing has clearly demonstrated that the same pair of swallows will nest at the same site, over several years, particularly if breeding has been successful.

While swallows may have arrived later this year, the passage of swifts around the Norfolk coast commenced about a week earlier than usual. This was no doubt related to the temporary, but nonetheless welcome, period of warm weather, before the wind once more swung round to the northerly quarter.

However, it won't be until mid-May that we can reasonably expect to see three species that typically arrive after most summer migrants have already returned. Firstly, spotted flycatchers, which have sadly declined in recent years, and are often found breeding in close association with man, frequently choosing to nest in a creeper or other shrub growing on the side of a house.

Secondly, nightjars, or "goat-suckers", that breed on heaths and in forestry clearings, although it probably won't be until the balmy days of June, that we can expect to hear their strange, churring songs as dusk falls. Incidentally, the name "goat-sucker" arose because of a superstition, dating back as far as Aristotle, that nightjars drank milk directly from goat's udders. Even the bird's generic Latin name, *Caprimulgus*, refers to this false suggestion.

Finally, one of East Anglia's rarest breeding birds, the honey buzzard, is one of the last to arrive. The species winters in equatorial Africa and does depend on fine weather for its long migratory journey. This is just one of several species of birds of prey that can be seen from the Raptor Watch Point at Swanton Novers, which is well worth a visit in mid-summer.

Stubble is helping the survival of woodlarks

June 2001

In the last few years, the heaths of North Norfolk have once more hosted breeding woodlarks. The changes in the British population of this species admirably demonstrate the fluctuating numbers that occur in many birds over a period of years - in the case of the woodlark, spanning at least two centuries! Again, in common with many other species, these fluctuations are often the direct result of man's influence on the countryside.

In Norfolk, woodlarks were widely distributed on heaths and common land prior to the General Enclosure Act of 1801, but became scarce and very localised during the next hundred years, as more Enclosure Acts were introduced. For reasons not fully understood, the first half of the twentieth century saw a steady increase in numbers, particularly in Breckland, but as before this trend was once again reversed. On this occasion the reduction coincided with an expansion of agriculture in parts of the Brecks, coupled with the absence of intense grazing by rabbits following the outbreak of myxomatosis in 1953.

As a result, by 1973, woodlarks were recorded from only four localities in Breckland, until man's activities fortuitously worked in their favour. As the conifers planted in the 1920s and 1930s matured, and were felled and harvested, open land was created. Once again this provided an ideal habitat for breeding woodlarks, and their numbers have even surpassed earlier estimates. Hopefully, as the mature trees are cropped in rotation, prime woodlark habitat should now always be available. It is likely that birds from this healthy Breckland population have spread into other parts of East Anglia, such as those that first recolonised the heathlands of North Norfolk, a few years ago.

In May, I was listening to the delightful sound of the cascading yodel of a woodlark, as it advertised its territory on a heath only a few miles from home. On a return visit, a few days later, I found another pair escorting their three, well-grown young, as they foraged amongst the short, heathland vegetation.

Until recently, East Anglian's breeding woodlarks were thought to be migratory, as very few are ever seen in winter. However, recent research by the British Trust for Ornithology has revealed small, but significant numbers on Breckland stubble fields during the winter months. This could help to explain the very early arrival of singing birds on some breeding sites, occasionally even as early as January. This provides further evidence of the importance of barley and wheat stubbles to the winter survival of yet another species.

Annual trip to fen is always a delight

June 2000

In late May, I made my annual summer visit to the RSPB's reserve at Strumpshaw Fen. Being an internationally important wetland reserve for birds, plants and insects, it is of great interest to all those with a love of natural history.

I well remember my first visit to the area in the late 1970s and thinking what tremendous potential there was for it to become one of the premier wetland sites in Norfolk. Now over 20 years on, thanks to the efforts of all the staff and volunteers, Strumpshaw Fen is a fine example of just what can be achieved with appropriate management.

While walking along the trail, which skirts the extensive reed-beds and meres, it's easy to forget that the hustle and bustle of the centre of Norwich is only a few miles away.

The reed-beds were alive with the chattering songs of reed warblers, the occasional bird climbing to the top of a reed stem, before sliding down again, much like a fireman on his pole.

The Yare Valley, where the reserve lies, is one of the best places in Norfolk, in which to see the elusive Cetti's warbler. There was no difficulty in locating this small, scrub-loving bird, from its sudden, loud bursts of brief song, in the bushes adjacent to the path. But actually seeing one, was an entirely different matter. Although I was fortunate enough to catch a brief glimpse, a friend from Essex who was with me, wasn't so lucky and in fact has never actually set eyes on one, despite having heard them on many occasions!

At least two pairs of marsh harriers graced the skies and we were treated to several spectacular aerial food passes - during which prey was passed from the talons of the male to the female. Continuing the raptor theme, a fine hobby was chasing low over the reeds, no doubt in pursuit of the first few dragonflies of the year. Amongst the dragonflies on the wing, which had managed to avoid the attentions of the hobbies, were several black-tailed skimmers, the males with their distinctive black-tipped blue abdomens, and the rare Norfolk hawker, which is only found in the Broads area of Norfolk and Suffolk.

Butterflies were also taking advantage of the warm, early summer sunshine and although we saw several brimstones, the other yellow butterflies that we were hoping to see, the swallowtails, remained elusive.

But perhaps the most surprising sighting of the day was a handsome drake mandarin which flew into the reserve with a small flight of mallard.

A warbler that's often heard, but rarely seen

October 2001

One of the great joys of birdwatching is coming across the unexpected. No matter how many times one has walked along a regularly used track, there is always the chance that something different may be found.

So it was at Kelling Water Meadows a couple of weeks ago. Suddenly from a patch of reeds and scattered bushes, the unmistakable explosive song of a Cetti's warbler broke the silence. Once heard, it is such a distinct song that it's unlikely to be forgotten. In the same way that a yellowhammer's song can be rendered as "A little bit of bread and no cheeeese", the Collins Bird Guide suggests that the song of the Cetti's warbler translates as "Listen!...What's my name?...Cetti-Cetti-Cetti-that's it!", and this indeed is a very good way to remember it.

It's perhaps just as well that Cetti's do have a loud and distinct song, for they are great skulkers, spending most of their time well hidden in the undergrowth or feeding dunnock-like on the ground under dense cover. Occasionally, however, they do sit briefly in the open displaying their warm chestnut upperparts and greyish-white underparts. They always seem to be on the move and are fairly aggressive little birds, so that the most frequent view is of one chasing another bird through cover, when their longish, rounded tail and rather short wings become apparent.

Unlike most warblers, they are resident in England throughout the year, and so their numbers may be severely affected by periods of prolonged hard winter weather. Another unusual characteristic is their polygamous breeding behaviour, with the males pairing up with several females. Not surprisingly, therefore, the pair bond is not very strong, and the two sexes only tend to associate for courtship and mating (sounds familiar, doesn't it?).

While the female constructs the nest, the male just keeps a watchful eye on the proceedings, and once completed shows little further interest. Occasional males do, however, help to feed the young, although at one nest under observation a male was once seen to approach the nest with food, and then eat it himself!

It was as recently as 1972 that Cetti's warblers first bred in the British Isles, and two years later were found nesting in Norfolk. At the present time about 100 male Cetti's are recorded in the county during the spring and summer, with the stronghold in the valleys of the Rivers Yare and Bure. The occasional birds that turn up in North Norfolk during the autumn and winter are thought to be birds from this Broadland breeding population.

Bath time for birds is quite a sight

August 1999

Last week I spent some time watching sand martins bathing in a small freshwater pool behind the shingle bank at Weybourne. Bathing is just one of the many aspects of feather care to which all birds must attend.

Sand martins, in common with other hirundines (members of the swallow family) and swifts, bathe by dipping into the surface of the water, in a kamikaze-like fashion. By timing their descent to perfection, they are able to skim the surface of the water, so that their body is sufficiently wet, before their momentum and a few well-timed flaps, lift them clear and back into the air.

Of course, the commonest method of bathing, and the one most often seen at garden bird baths and around the edges of ponds, involves so-called "stand-in" bathing. In this situation birds such as blackbirds, robins or house sparrows, ruffle up their feathers and repeatedly dip the head and breast into the water, while shaking the body and flapping the wings.

An interesting combination of the two methods is shown by some species of ducks, for instance teal. When undertaken by several birds together it makes for fascinating watching, as the ducks flap across the surface of the water or make short flights before diving headlong beneath the surface. This is often repeated several times in a short space of time.

The black-headed gulls on the beach at Sheringham clearly prefer to bath in freshwater rather than the sea. At low tide they gather at the outfall at the east end of the promenade, to bath and drink from the freshwater flowing down from the beck on Beeston Common.

Several years ago I remember watching a collared dove rain bathing, during a shower. It sat on a fence fully exposed to the heavy rainfall, with feathers ruffled, wings raised and tail spread, clearly revelling in the experience. I was fascinated to see the same behaviour repeated by several species of birds, both large and small, on a recent birding trip to Trinidad. In a part of the world where tropical storms are commonplace and standing water can be hard to find, it clearly was a case of making the most of the prevailing conditions.

Returning to the sand martins at Weybourne, after several plunges into the water, each bird flew up to a nearby fence to dry out and preen. Thus completing their "wash and brush-up"!

Bird that brightens up the summer

June 2001

Surely one of the most attractive of our summer migrants must be the yellow wagtail; sadly it is becoming far less common as a breeding bird. The dazzling, daffodil-yellow underparts of the male in spring, makes it an unmistakable bird, feeding as it often does in areas of short grass. Female yellow wagtails are far less distinct, retaining the olive green upperparts, but often being pale buff below.

Although the first birds of the spring pass through East Anglia in early April, the main passage is not until May, when small flocks can often be seen feeding around the feet of cattle, especially on grazing marshes along the coast. Strangely enough, apart from wagtails, few other birds appear to take advantage of the insects that are disturbed by grazing cattle.

It's always worth checking any group of yellow wagtails, especially in spring, for males of the other European races. British breeding males generally show a yellowish-green crown, matching the upperparts, whereas the other races have bluish or grey heads, making them even more attractive. Two of these varieties are recorded annually in East Anglia. The commonest, the blue-headed wagtail, breeds in most of continental Europe, and even occasionally in Britain, and is recognised by its blue-grey head displaying a prominent white supercilium (stripe above the eye). Whereas the grey-headed wagtail, from northern Fennoscandia, differs in having a darker grey head, especially around the ear coverts, and lacks the paler supercilium.

During the breeding season, yellow wagtails traditionally frequent damp meadows, where they construct well-concealed nests in grassy tussocks. Their decline as a breeding species in Norfolk can be attributed to a combination of wetland drainage and overgrazing that results in too short a sward in which they can safely nest. This summer, however, I have also found them nesting around the edges of fields of spring-sown crops.

As long ago as 1924, Emma Turner, writing in her book, Broadland Birds, blamed the initial decline on the advent of the motor car. The favoured Broadland hay-meadows having become overgrown with rank vegetation, as the hay crop was no longer needed as fodder for the horses that pulled the London buses and cabs. It seems ironic that exactly the opposite situation now exists!

After breeding, yellow wagtails gather into flocks once again, prior to their autumn migration, roosting at night in reed-beds, along with pied wagtails and swallows. Most have departed these shores by late September, taking several weeks to reach their wintering areas in tropical Africa, and thus completing their annual cycle.

Delights along the coastal footpath

June 2001

Despite the brisk westerly wind, it was a delightfully warm and sunny day last week, as I set off west along the Peddars Way and Norfolk Coast Path from the National Trust car park at Morston Quay. The blue sky was reflected in the waters of Blakeney Pit, slowly filling with the incoming tide, and the first sailing dinghies were tacking their way up Morston Creek, their sails filled by the stiff breeze.

The wide expanse of saltings, criss-crossed by narrow channels, is the home of numerous pairs of redshanks during the summer months, and the agitated alarm calls of several birds indicated the presence of young redshanks amongst the salt marsh vegetation. Occasional little terns, recognised by their small size and yellow, black-tipped bills, hovered over the shallow water, as the creeks slowly filled. Looking back towards the quayside, I could see the queues of visitors beginning to form, ready to board the seal boats that would transport them out to the Point.

At this time of year, the patches of gorse bordering the coastal path are in full splendour, the bright yellow flowers providing a perfect background to a cock linnet that was perched on top, uttering its simple but pleasant song. The spiky leaves of the gorse provide admirable protection for the nests of linnets and whitethroats, both of which breed commonly along this stretch of the coastal path.

At one point, a highly mimetic songster, incorporating the trill of a linnet, the spink of a chaffinch and the scolding call of a blackbird, had me fooled, until it flew up from a patch of bramble and parachuted back down singing - a sedge warbler, but one with a most unusual song.

After a mile or so, I had reached Stiffkey Fen, a freshwater marsh, on the landward side of the sea wall, incorporating islands and reeds. Created several years ago by Lord Buxton and English Nature, it is a fine example of what can be achieved by sympathetic and appropriate land management. Despite the presence of several hundred greylag geese, which are undoubtedly causing a problem, a wide variety of species were breeding on the reserve. Amongst the colony of black-headed gulls were a few pairs of avocets, while broods of young coot, mallard and shelduck were already in evidence. A late common sandpiper teetering along the muddy fringe of the shallow water provided evidence that spring passage was still under way, as did the swifts that flew west throughout the morning.

Shovelers, spoonbills and skimmers

November 2000

Waterfowl show a wide variety of bill shapes, for example the majority of surface-feeding duck all share the same basic design with a rather broad, flat, elongated bill, but it is taken to extreme in the shoveler, as its name suggests. In this species the bill is particularly long and gives the duck a very distinct and somewhat ungainly profile. But it does make an ideal "shovel" with which to scoop up food from the water surface, as it swims around feeding.

Diving duck that catch fish underwater, such as the goosander and red-breasted merganser, have long, narrow bills, with teeth-like serrations along the sides, enabling them to get a better grip on their slippery prey. For this reason, the group as a whole are known as sawbills.

The strange and well-known shape of the puffin's bill is also partly an adaptation to its underwater exploits. Puffins often have to fly many miles from their nesting burrows to fishing grounds far out to sea. The size and shape of their bills allows them to carry home up to ten small fish or sand eels, arranged head to tail crosswise along the length of the bill.

Among the wading birds, surface-feeders show a great diversity from the delicate, upturned bill of the avocet to the very long, flat spoon-shaped bill of the aptly named spoonbill. Both of these very different designs allow the birds to sweep the surface of the water, from side to side, and filter out invertebrates; and in the case of the spoonbill, catch small fish and even frogs.

Outside Europe, a group of birds known as skimmers, have developed an even stranger method of feeding from the water surface. Related to terns, all three species of skimmer are black above and white below, but are characterised by their unique bills. The lower mandible is longer than the upper and it skims the surface of the water as it flies along, snapping up shrimps and small fish.

But perhaps the strangest of all are the pelicans. The capacity of their outrageously oversized bills being increased by the distensible pouch that hangs below, as has been immortalised in the words of Dixon Lannier Merritt -

A wonderful bird is the pelican,
his bill can hold more than his belican.
He can take in his beak,
food enough for a week.
But I'm damned if I see how the helican.

Birds that can sound almost human

June 2000

For many hundreds, indeed thousands, of years, starlings have been renowned for their ability to mimic the human voice. One in Northamptonshire is known to have had a vocabulary of 30 words. The Latin author, Pliny, in ancient times wrote of "some avian classics scholars of his acquaintance imitating Greek and Latin ... which practised diligently and spoke new phrases every day". While Mozart owned a starling for three years which had incorporated into its song a tune remarkably similar to part of one of its owner's piano concertos! The greatest bird mimics, however, are mynah birds, themselves related to starlings. One of the most famous being called "TV", which lived in New York and had a vocabulary of 500 words, thus earning itself a place in the Guinness Book of Records.

But why do birds copy the human voice? They apparently never do so in the wild. In captivity, they are in close contact with humans and often isolated from other members of their own species. By learning to vocalise they appear to appreciate that it increases the attention they receive. For instance, parrots often start to talk when their owners leave the room, as if by talking, they're trying to get them back.

In the wild, starlings are certainly one of our greatest mimics, readily picking up the calls of other birds with which they come into contact. Around the Norfolk coast, it is not unusual to hear starlings on the rooftops sounding like redshanks, oystercatchers or curlews. In the West Country, the distinct mewing cry of a buzzard, is often uttered by starlings.

Amongst our woodland birds, the great tit probably has the greatest repertoire, and more often than not is responsible for producing a sound that is not instantly recognisable. On occasions, their calls can be almost indistinguishable from marsh tits and coal tits, while they are also capable of producing a sound very much like the "chink" of a chaffinch.

But, without doubt, the greatest mimic in Europe is a summer visitor, the marsh warbler. On average, a male will incorporate into its rich and varied song, the calls of no less than 76 other species. Of these about half will be of birds it has heard during the summer in Europe and the rest during the winter in Africa. So if you hear bird-song coming from the middle of a bush, that sounds like a linnet, nightingale, little tern, blue tit, sedge warbler and woodlark, all rolled into one, it's probably a marsh warbler producing it!

Amazing display of colourful blooms

June 2000

Living right on the doorstep of The National Trust's property at Sheringham Park, I am naturally a regular visitor to the cliffs, parkland and woods, which comprise this fine estate. Designed by the great landscape gardener, Humphrey Repton, in the early nineteenth century, Sheringham Park became Repton's "most favourite work" and he also stated "...that Sheringham possesses more natural beauty and local advantages, than any place I have ever seen". Mind you, he was probably biased having lived in the nearby village of Sustead; although I'm sure that many of the past and present residents of Sheringham would entirely agree with him, myself included!

A visit to the park in late May or early June, is always a treat, to witness the truly magnificent display of flowering rhododendrons and azaleas. Their vibrant colours from various shades of purple, through reds to oranges and yellows, are a great tribute to the skills of several generations of Upchers who lived at Sheringham Hall and who acquired over many years, such a varied collection. Dark bowers leading tunnel-like through the ancient rhododendrons, guide the visitor to two viewing platforms, from the top of which the blossoms can be seen in their full glory.

Despite having been introduced from Asia over two hundred years ago, as game cover in woods, rhododendrons are still only sparingly used by most British birds. In winter, the dense foliage provides good cover for roosting blackbirds, green-finches and chaffinches, but rhododendrons are rarely used as nesting or feeding sites. Pheasants, of course, also originate from Asia and thus the choice of an Asian shrub to provide game cover, was readily accepted by them.

During a recent walk through Sheringham Park, I was interested to find a concentration of territory-holding song thrushes (Plate 3), in the rhododendron-lined drive leading to the Hall. As with pheasants, there are a large number of species of thrush living in Asia and I wonder whether this is why song thrushes appear to have adapted more readily to this introduced type of shrub.

Entering the parkland along the main drive, we walked towards Sheringham Hall, nestling on the leeward side of Oak Wood. Here, not only does it face south but it is also sheltered from the storms of the North Sea. I couldn't believe our luck, for as we approached, the unmistakable fluty calls of a golden oriole were clearly audible from the canopy of oaks behind the Hall. But unfortunately, despite its bright colours, we failed to catch a glimpse of it in the dense leaf cover.

The balmy days of summer

Wren keen to help out with nest duties

June 2000

Of the many phone calls that I have received recently about birds, three were of particular interest.

The first, from Martin Austin of Cromer, concerned a great tit and treecreeper apparently using the same nest box in his garden. This was a most unusual report and I was keen to see, what I believe would have been a unique occurrence. To be fair, when I arrived at his house, he did say that the second occupant may have been a wren and not a treecreeper, but this did not detract from my interest.

The nest box, sited on a tree in his front garden, was a typical tit box with a single round opening, and as we stood there, sure enough a wren flew in carrying a bill full of food. From inside the box could be heard the hungry calls of the nestlings and after a few seconds out flew the wren. This was repeated several times over the course of the next ten minutes and then a male great tit arrived, and rather more timidly entered the box to feed the young. On carefully lifting the lid of the box, I was able to see that it held a single nest containing four young great tits, almost on the point of fledging. So whatever was the wren up to?

This sort of behaviour has been recorded before and appears to involve birds whose own nestlings have been killed, but which still possess the maternal (or paternal) desire to feed young. Presumably the wren had heard the young great tits calling from within the box and instinctively had been unable to overcome the drive to feed them. The natural parents in such situations, appear to readily accept this additional help, and indeed from my brief observations at this nest, seemed to be doing far less work than the adoptive parent!

The second phone call was from a lady near Aylsham who said that a pair of fulfers was feeding two young in her garden. I assumed that she meant "English fulfers", that is mistle thrushes, but no, she and her husband were sure they were fieldfares. As this species has never been proved to breed in Norfolk, I readily drove over to check out her observations. Unfortunately, they had been mistaken and the birds were indeed mistle thrushes.

Finally, I was asked to examine the corpse of a large bird with a hooked bill, found on the tide-line, which was thought to be an exotic South American species. Sadly, it was just a very smelly cockerel!

Rabbits are only doing what comes naturally

November 1999

Don't blame the rabbit for the current population explosion, after all they're only doing what comes naturally!

Rabbits are believed to have evolved in Iberia, and probably first appeared in Britain during the twelth century, introduced by, who else, but man. In southern Europe, almost 40 species of mammals and birds prey on rabbits. No wonder then that the species has become such a prolific breeder, simply in order to survive. Each female rabbit produces about ten young annually, although many more than that will be conceived, only to die after a few days and be reabsorbed in the womb. Whilst still suckling, and on occasions within twelve hours of birth, she will mate again, and thus the cycle is rapidly repeated.

At Weybourne, where there is a large rabbit population, I cursed their constant attacks on willow saplings I planted ten years ago. Although the trees got off to a very poor start due to the salt spray, biting winds, late spring frosts and the rabbits, they are now well over 20ft high.

All animals undergo natural fluctuations in population levels and rabbits are no exception. The last few years have certainly seen an enormous increase in numbers, but at Weybourne a particularly virulent strain of myxomatosis is now beginning to exert its effect. Never before have I found so many dead and dying rabbits as this year. This is bound to have a significant effect next summer. During the 1950s' epidemic of myxomatosis it was estimated that 99% of the population succumbed.

Rabbits, however, are not necessarily bad news. The resulting close cropped turf in Breckland is favoured by stone curlew, while their burrows provide nesting holes for wheatears. Rabbits also provide a source of food for stoats, weasels, foxes and buzzards, although all of these might be considered to be vermin in certain areas.

Sir Harry Johnston writing in his classic book British Mammals in 1903 stated "In a natural state of affairs the increase of the rabbit in Europe and the British Isles would be kept in check by the proportionate increase of weasels, cats, foxes, buzzards, owls, and eagles; but when man, in his short-sightedness, exterminates these interesting beasts and birds, he must rely solely on his own efforts to keep down the devastations of rabbits and other rodents". Almost a hundred years on and it seems that we still havn't learnt our lesson!

Calls are the key to recognition for birds

July 2001

Many readers must have followed Professor Robert Winston's fascinating television programme "Child Of Our Time". The last in the present series discussed how it is possible to influence musical taste by playing music to an unborn child. He also demonstrated that even at six months of age, a child was still capable of remembering the music heard while in the womb. Such learning is of great importance in the world of birds.

On a recent visit to the RSPB's Titchwell Reserve I was interested to watch the reactions of the nestlings and their parents as the adult black-headed gulls returned to the breeding colony with food. Although young birds would run towards any adult with food, all except their parents, which instantly recognised their own young, ignored their begging. Apart from obvious size differences due to age, many of the young appeared identical, at least to my eyes. So how did the adults know which young to feed?

The recognition of individual calls features at a very early stage in many birds' lives. In some cases birds actually call while still in the egg, and this is exactly what happens with black-headed gulls and with most birds that breed in colonies. Towards the end of the period of incubation the well-grown chick, which is inside the egg, begins to call, and this sound is recognised by the parents as that of their own offspring. To them it is a unique call, which will allow them to identify their own chicks, when returning with food at a later date.

In the same way, guillemots flying back to their breeding ledges are able to identify their own egg from amongst, perhaps many hundreds, lying on the bare rocky ledge, by the call of the chick within the egg!

But returning to the theme of Professor Winston's programme, the unhatched chick also learns to recognise the calls of its parents. In fact it has been demonstrated that young gulls cannot beg for food unless previously exposed to maternal feeding calls before hatching. Certainly the fervour shown by the young gulls at Titchwell did increase noticeably as they approached their own parents.

Just in front of the hide, a female mallard and her four young ducklings were also demonstrating the importance of call recognition. Although only a couple of days old, the ducklings were swimming and feeding in an area up to 20 yards away from Mum, who was showing very little concern for her brood; but if danger threatened, her call was instantly recognised by the ducklings, which went scurrying back to her.

Community spirit in crèches of shelducks

July 2000
My recent article, about a wren helping to raise a brood of great tit nestlings, has resulted in two further interesting reports.

An EDP reader from Barnham Broom phoned to say that a pair of blue tits, nesting in a box in her garden, was also being assisted in parental duties by a wren. However, unlike the great tits at Cromer about which I wrote recently, her blue tits were not entirely happy with this intrusion and were actively aggressive towards the wren, which nevertheless continued to feed their young! Ray Jones of Old Catton also contacted me about a blue tit and a wren that were seen carrying nesting material into the same box in a friend's garden. At the peak of the activity, as one bird left the other entered! However, there was no evidence that either pair successfully occupied the nest box.

Long-tailed tits make delightful domed nests of moss and lichens, lined with feathers. The number of feathers used is amazing, as was demonstrated many years ago when six used nests were examined and found to contain between 985 and 2084 feathers, each one of which would have been taken individually into the nest! Long-tailed tits are one of the first birds to breed in spring, but unfortunately many of these early nests and clutches are destroyed by predators. Although some pairs may make a second nesting attempt, others will not. Instead they direct their efforts into helping other pairs of long-tailed tits raise their young. As the average brood size is 9-10, this additional help from one or two extra adult birds must be very welcome. Family parties of long-tailed tits are a common sight in mid-summer and they remain in these groups, often joining together with other families, until the following spring.

Another interesting example of parental assistance is shown by the moorhen, in which fully-grown youngsters from the first brood, help to care for the young of the second brood. Yet another strategy adopted by certain species, such as penguins, flamingos and shelducks, is the formation of crèches. The broods from several or many pairs of shelducks will amalgamate at suitable freshwater sites, forming groups of 100 or more ducklings, with just one or two adults in attendance. This arrangement enables all the rest of the adults to leave for their moulting grounds, where over a period of several weeks they remain flightless as their wing feathers are regrown. Traditionally, Norfolk's shelducks have moulted in the Heligoland Bight, but in recent years large numbers now gather in The Wash.

Nightjar - an East Anglian enigma

July 2000

The nightjar, with its strange nocturnal habits, is probably one of East Anglia's most enigmatic birds. Spending the winter months in sub-Saharan Africa, the first birds have generally returned to England by early May, although it is not until the end of the month that I normally start visiting my local heaths in search of them.

Although nightjars are often described as crepuscular, that is most active in the twilight hours of dusk and dawn, they do in fact fly and feed throughout the night. They are admirably adapted for catching flying insects in poor light, having unusually large eyes and very wide gapes. The width is further increased by the presence of strong rictal bristles at each corner of the gape, thus creating a large "funnel" in which flying moths and beetles can be readily caught.

Like owls they fly silently, but on long pointed wings, and it is from this wing shape that they are known by the alternative name of nighthawk. Being active at night, they sleep by day and their mottled grey-brown plumage provides superb camouflage as they rest on the ground, often amongst bracken, or stretched out reptilian-like along the branch of a tree.

To stand on one of the North Norfolk heaths, on a warm, still mid-summer evening just as dusk is falling, is an unforgettable experience. As the light fades, one begins to wonder if the nightjars are going to perform after all, then suddenly one is aware of that strange, low churring sound coming from somewhere in the distance, or is it near at hand? Such are their ventriloquial skills that it is often very hard to determine from whence the sound is emanating. Once one bird has started churring, others often join in. Occasionally, it is just possible through the fading light to make out the silhouette of a nightjar sitting on top of a gorse bush or the branch of one of the small birch trees. More often, a sighting consists of a male, recognised by white spots near the wing tips, flying ghost-like around in search of insects or performing his wing clapping display.

In recent years, the commercial felling of mature conifers, and the subsequent creation of clearfell areas and new plantations, has led to a steady increase in the breeding nightjar population of East Anglia. Many fascinating local names are used for nightjar, three in Norfolk being "scissor-grinder" and "razor-grinder", as well as "flying toad".

Migrant butterflies arrive from the south

July 2000
In mid-June I was delighted to find a clouded yellow butterfly flitting restlessly over the long grass, on the landward side of the Wiveton bank near Cley. Although it occasionally settled briefly, it was soon on the wing again and I have little doubt that it must have been a recent arrival from the Continent.

Between a large and small white butterfly in size, its upperwings were bright orangy-yellow with a fairly broad black border. It was the first that I had seen in East Anglia for a number of years, and its appearance was probably associated with the warm southerly winds that we had been enjoying for the previous few days.

Clouded yellows are not common in Britain and their presence depends on the arrival of migrants from mainland Europe. The species overwinters around the Mediterranean, from whence in spring, the butterflies migrate north to breed widely in central and northern Europe. It is the progeny of this generation which appears in variable numbers in the British Isles from late May onwards. In some years, notably 1877, 1947, 1955 and more recently 1983, large numbers have been recorded in Britain, but whether or not the year 2000 will become a "clouded yellow year" remains to be seen.

I can well remember standing on the sea front at Sheringham, many years ago, and watching in amazement as thousands upon thousands of large white butterflies flew steadfastly west, low over the waves. For several hundred yards offshore they were moving on a broad front, like small pieces of white paper being blown along in the wind. These, again, were migrants arriving from across the North Sea.

However, the two species of butterfly which arrive each summer in Britain, after migrating from southern Europe and even as far away as North Africa, are the red admiral and painted lady. This year, I had seen my first painted lady on the cliff-top fields at Sheringham, two weeks before my sighting of the clouded yellow. Since then they had become increasingly widespread and had been joined by a few red admirals.

In common with birds, butterflies use the sun as a compass while migrating, often flying into a light wind to obtain lift. But unlike birds, the same butterflies do not make the return journey. If it is attempted, it is one of the next generation that undertakes it. Although occasional red admirals do survive the winter in England, painted ladies have probably never done so, as they contain insufficient sorbitol in their blood, which acts as an antifreeze in cold weather.

Hobby is a true master of the air

July 2001

All birds of prey are exciting to watch, but of those that breed in East Anglia, the hobby is undoubtedly my favourite. With its long, pointed scythe-like wings and dashing flight, it truly is a master of the air. Even at a distance, its characteristic flight, combined with the slate-grey upperparts, darkly streaked underparts and distinct white throat, make it comparatively easy to identify. At closer range, the reddish-brown "trousers" and undertail coverts are additional features to look out for.

Traditionally hobbies were associated with the downs and heathlands of the southern counties of England, but from the late 1970s a noticeable northward expansion in range occurred. Although it remains a scarce breeding bird in Norfolk, with probably no more than 20 pairs annually, it's certainly on the increase.

The hobby is a summer visitor to Europe with the majority of birds returning from the African tropics in May. The early summer is probably the best time to see them, as they rather lazily fly above reed-beds and areas of open water in pursuit of dragonflies and other flying insects; clutching the prey in their claws, they then proceed to eat it while still in flight. Several of the Norfolk Wildlife Trust's wetland reserves host these fine birds throughout the summer.

Fortunately for the birds, it is never easy to locate their exact breeding sites. They can be remarkably unobtrusive during the egg laying and incubation stages, nesting in disused nests in trees, often those of carrion crows. Although they are largely insectivorous for most of the year, they turn to bird prey once the young have hatched in mid-July.

It is at this time of year, that their remarkable manoeuvrability in the air becomes apparent. Hunting very often in the early morning or at dusk, they will fly casually around, often behind some trees, before suddenly streaking off towards a flock of swallows or martins. Total panic sets in, as the hobby wheels around, twisting this way and that in pursuit of its intended victim. Their speed and agility in the air even allows them to catch swifts, while other recorded prey species in Norfolk have included a little tern at Scolt Head, bats at Felbrigg, and peacock and small tortoiseshell butterflies.

But perhaps the most spectacular sight is when a hobby appears at a hirundine roost in late summer. I shall never forget seeing one flying low and fast over the reedbed at the NWT reserve at Cley on a balmy August evening, being pursued by a screaming host of swallows, with the glow of the setting sun visible over the distant horizon.

Summer is a busy season for parents

August 1999

As summer progresses, our gardens, hedgerows and woods become alive with the calls of young birds, begging for food from their overworked parents. Some of the most persistent are the recently fledged starlings (Plate 3), in their distinctive plain brown plumage as compared to the iridescent black attire of the adult birds. Of particular interest is the fact that starlings in breeding plumage are one of the few species in which the old adage "blue for boys and pink for girls" is found in nature. Look carefully at adult starlings in spring and early summer and you will be able to recognise the males by the sky-blue colour at the base of the bill, compared with the pink of the females.

Many species of birds in Britain have more than one brood during the course of the summer, but not so the members of the tit family, which are generally single brooded. This is compensated for by large clutch sizes - even up to 15 eggs in the blue tit! Both blue and great tits time their egg laying, so that hatching and subsequent fledging of the brood coincide with the glut of moth caterpillars in May and early June, upon which the young are fed. What more delightful scene is there than a row of young blue tits lined up on a branch, constantly calling to attract the attention of their ever-busy parents. Surely the original primary school chorus line!

Also at this time of year, family parties of long-tailed tits are a familiar sight in the countryside and even in the larger gardens. Here in Sheringham, a group of about a dozen long-tailed tits has been passing through my garden daily for the last couple of weeks. Almost invariably the birds follow a similar route visiting the same bushes and trees on each occasion, suggesting that it is the same family party each day in its constant search for food. As with the other tits, small insects are the main prey items, and in summer, long-tailed tits are rarely recorded visiting garden bird tables or feeding on peanuts.

Perhaps surprisingly, caterpillars are also the main food item collected by chaffinches to feed to their offspring, whereas outside the breeding season, chaffinches feed almost exclusively on seeds. These include the seeds of many of our common wild plants, spilt cereal grain or in the years when the beech crop is good, on the fallen mast. Not only are caterpillars easier to find in the summer but they are also more nutritious for the rapidly-growing young birds.

Distinctive "buzz" of the curious dragonfly

August 1999

Although many birdwatchers nowadays also show an interest, and very often considerable expertise, in other aspects of the local fauna and flora, dragonflies have traditionally been known as the "birdwatcher's insects". In many ways their identification is fairly easy, provided you can get close enough to see their individual features. Only just over 40 species occur regularly in the United Kingdom, of which about 30 have been recorded in Norfolk (Plate 4).

I can well remember as a youngster while fishing, trying to keep well away from dragonflies believing that they could sting. Of course this is quite untrue, although the larger species are capable of giving an unpleasant nip with their biting mouth parts.

Dragonflies, and their smaller cousins damselflies, are important indicators of water quality. Very few species tolerate pollution, an exception being the common and widespread blue-tailed damselfly. At only an inch long, the males are readily recognised by their black bodies with a thin blue stripe on either side of the thorax, and a distinctive short blue segment near the tip of the tail. The species is on the wing throughout the summer from mid-May onwards.

Any area of clean freshwater from garden ponds to the Broads and Breckland meres, as well as slow flowing rivers, are attractive to dragonflies. If you stand quietly on the edge of such an area of water it won't be long before an inquisitive dragonfly "buzzes" you. It's simply checking what has entered its territory. Its great manoeuvrability and turn of speed, allows the dragonfly to feed on flies, moths, butterflies or indeed any other flying insect, small enough for it to handle. However, not surprisingly, insects with stings, such as wasps, tend to be avoided!

The adult dragonflies, which we see flying over water or along a woodland ride, are only the final stage of a long period of development. As flying insects they live for a maximum of only two to three months, and many for only a couple of weeks. But prior to their emergence as adults, they will have spent one to two years or even longer as underwater larvae.

There are now many excellent books on dragonfly identification and behaviour, but for use in the field Steve Brooks' Field Guide to Dragonflies and Damselflies of Great Britain and Ireland is hard to better and easily fits in a pocket.

Keep a lookout for stock doves

November 2001

Fellow columnist, Percy Trett, recently described the dramatic increase in the wood-pigeon population in East Anglia, in recent years.

Woodpigeons actually declined in numbers during the 1960s and early 1970s due to a combination of cold winters, chemical seed dressings, weed control and the switch to autumn-sown cereal crops. However, research by the British Trust for Ornithology has indeed demonstrated a doubling of the breeding population in the last 25 years. Traditionally, woodpigeons have been late summer breeders, but by breeding earlier they are now able to exploit the recent abundance of oil-seed rape.

Another widespread, but less well known, member of the pigeon family is the stock dove. Like the woodpigeon, this species too has recovered steadily from the pesticide kills of the 1950s and early 1960s, and the British population has increased by 85% during the same period. But I wonder how many readers have ever knowingly seen a stock dove? They are the sort of birds that once you have tuned in to their characteristics, you will recognise them on most countryside walks.

About the size of feral pigeons but more compact, they always seem to have more rounded wings in flight, at least to my eyes. On occasions, as they fly away, they can look surprisingly like a small bird of prey. In flight they are uniformly grey apart from black wing tips and a dark trailing edge, lacking the white wing flash of woodpigeons and the white rump of feral pigeons. When seen perched at fairly close range, with the sun glinting on their iridescent purplish-green neck patch, they are transformed into surprisingly attractive birds.

Unlike woodpigeons, they nest in holes in trees or if unavailable in old buildings. At Weybourne, the old derelict wartime gun emplacements provide many suitable ledges, while some even nest on the ground in the old pillboxes. Ground nesting also occurs in old rabbit burrows in the Brecks. During the winter, stock doves gather into flocks to forage on the open fields, often in company with woodpigeons. Although odd stock doves can be found feeding amongst the pigeons, larger parties tend to remain slightly apart and they usually fly off in single species' flocks. Although stock doves are found throughout much of rural Norfolk during the summer, they do seem to desert certain parts of the county in winter.

If you keep your eyes open, you're bound to add this species to the list of birds that you regularly recognise.

Not all birds show maternal instincts

July 2001
I wonder how many readers have stopped to consider the very obvious differences between a day-old chick of a blackbird and that of a farmyard chicken?

In the case of the former, it is hatched blind, virtually naked and totally dependent on its parents for both warmth and food. Young of this type are known as altricial and are the norm for most passerine birds. It is in these species, that the parents make a well-constructed nest in which the young can grow safely over the course of a few weeks. If a nest containing young, only a few days old, is examined, one is often confronted by a set of enormous gapes, opened wide in expectation. At this stage, the young are no more than specialised food-processing machines!

Compare these helpless birds with those of a chicken or lapwing, of a similar age. Such young that are comparatively well developed at the time of hatching are called precocial and the eggs from which they hatch tend to be larger for the size of the adult bird. At birth, their eyes are open, they are well feathered and within a few hours are able to run around, even making attempts to feed themselves.

Young lapwings, for instance, are of course dependent to a certain extent on their parents. Initially they are shown how to feed, by picking suitable food items from the surface of the ground, as is well-known from the actions of a clucking mother hen as she fusses around her newly-hatched brood. Certainly during the first couple of days, lapwing chicks will also snuggle beneath one of their parents for protection or warmth, although they will very soon learn to run to any other available cover and crouch, motionless at the first sign of danger.

Absence of any parental care is taken to extreme in the Megapodes, a group of chicken-like birds from the Australasian Region, which lay their eggs under piles of sand or rotting vegetation that provide sufficient heat for incubation. Even after hatching, the young are totally alone and will run away from their parents, if they do happen to see them!

In between these two extremes, there are groups of birds that show characteristics of both, such as the herons and the birds of prey. Although they are hatched with their eyes open and with a good covering of down, they still remain in the nest for several weeks. Young such as these are also called nidicolous (nest-dwelling) as opposed to nidifugous (nest-fleeing), which are another couple of useful words for crossword enthusiasts!

Magical Cley - the jewel in the crown

August 1999

Suddenly the peace and tranquillity of the scene was transformed into chaos, as hundreds, perhaps thousands, of birds took flight. There seemed to be no pattern to their noisy wheeling as they flew around in panic - a swirling mass of geese, ducks and waders. The cause of this sudden commotion remained a mystery. It was almost certainly a bird of prey flying high over the Cley Marsh, which is undoubtedly the jewel in the crown of the reserves owned by the Norfolk Wildlife Trust.

Early August is one of the best and most challenging times to visit the reserve. Waders from their breeding grounds in northern Europe and Iceland are passing through on their way south, many of which will overwinter in Africa.

On this particular day, the most numerous were black-tailed godwits, many still resplendent with their beautiful rufous-orange breasts. Some were probing the mud with their long straight bills, others were preening, while some were apparently asleep. A few greenshank with their long, slightly upturned bills were present on the reserve, occasionally uttering their very distinctive, ringing call "tew-tew-tew", as they flew from one scrape to another. Delicate spotted redshanks, their pale grey plumage mottled with black, the last remnants of their breeding dress, graced the North Scrape.

The presence of mud-fringed freshwater pools, grazing marshes and reed-beds always prove attractive to birds (and birdwatchers), but what makes Cley so special is its juxtaposition to the North Sea. It truly is on the cross-roads of bird migration. However, the rich mosaic of habitats found at Cley is no accident. It is largely due to the imagination and management skills of Billy Bishop, warden of Cley Reserve for over 40 years. Since 1978 his son, Bernard, has been continuing this fine tradition and caring for the reserve to the same high standards. Thankfully, the threat of serious flooding, following North Sea storms, has been averted, by the plans to create a mud bank a couple of hundred yards to the south of the present shingle bank.

Throughout the summer, visitors to the area have been able to enjoy the spectacle of marsh harriers sailing effortlessly over the extensive reed-beds. The bittern has been heard booming regularly and has been seen by those fortunate enough to be in the right place at the right time. While avocets have continued to dominate the scrapes with their highly territorial behaviour.

Long may birds and birdwatchers be able to enjoy the delights of this magical place.

Moult is a demanding experience for birds

July 2000

The one unique feature of birds is their feathers, a characteristic possessed by no other living group. Feathers have a variety of functions, including heat retention, camouflage and display. However, their rather delicate structure does mean that they suffer from abrasion and need to be replaced at regular intervals. For most species, this feather replacement occurs once a year during their annual moult. Feather moult is extremely demanding in energy terms and generally does not overlap with either breeding or migration, although there are exceptions.

One of the reasons for the very obvious silence, which greets the woodland visitor in late summer, is the fact that many birds are in active moult and directing their energy towards this important activity. The adults of most of our passerines (small, perching birds) will undergo a complete moult as soon as their parental duties are completed in late summer. This involves replacing all the head, body, wing and tail feathers in sequence. Only one or two flight feathers in each wing will be missing at any one time, thus ensuring that the bird does not become flightless.

Many of our summer visitors, such as the blackcap, chiffchaff and redstart, also undertake a full moult immediately after breeding and before they begin their journey south in autumn. Others, like the garden warbler and swallow, wait until after they have arrived in their winter quarters. This is taken to the extreme in the willow warbler, which has two annual moults, one before autumn migration and a second after arriving in Africa, the only European-breeding passerine to do so. It is thought that these different strategies are related to the distances travelled in autumn.

By contrast, the vast majority of juvenile birds do not undergo a complete moult during their first autumn, simply replacing the head, body and wing covert feathers. This is well shown by the changes from the speckled plumage of a young robin, to the gradual appearance of the more familiar orange breast. As so often occurs in nature, however, there are a few exceptions to this rule, for example juvenile skylarks, starlings and house sparrows all have a complete moult in autumn, and are virtually identical to their parents by the time that winter comes round.

Much of our present knowledge about moult comes from the Moult Enquiry started in 1960 by the British Trust for Ornithology, the data being gathered from birds that had been caught for ringing.

Disastrous summer for our partridges

August 2000

The dreadful weather this summer will almost certainly have had a disastrous effect on many of our ground-nesting birds, perhaps none more so than on our partridges. Indeed, during my many visits to farmland this summer, I did not see a single brood of young partridges.

Sadly, the English or grey partridge (which was formerly known as the common partridge) has declined dramatically during the last 50 years, with the national population down by about 80 per cent. Traditionally, north-west Norfolk has been the stronghold for the species in the county, and this is once again being demonstrated during fieldwork for the Norfolk Bird Atlas. This is almost certainly due to the dedicated management in that part of Norfolk that ensures shootable surpluses, although this summer's weather may well upset the balance.

Nationally, the marked decline has been attributed to the increased use of herbicides which remove the weeds that are fed on by insects, on which the young grey partridges themselves feed during the first two weeks of life. The problem is then compounded by the summer use of insecticide sprays, as well as predation by crows and foxes.

Although the larger, French or red-legged partridges have also declined for the same reasons in recent years, they are still reasonably widespread and numerous throughout East Anglia. Originally introduced from the Continent into Suffolk in the late 1700s, the population is still boosted by annual releases of hand-reared birds. Strangely enough, red-legged partridges became unpopular as game birds during the nineteenth century. This was partly because they were too shy and too strong on the wing to be shot in large numbers by the average gun! As a result, gamekeepers were asked to destroy the nests and treat the birds as vermin.

There are several reasons why red-legs are tending to prosper, compared with grey partridges. Firstly, they are more tolerant of wooded landscapes - indeed it is not unusual for them to be flushed from woodland edges or along rides. Secondly, the newly-hatched young are less dependent on insect food, more readily taking grain; and thirdly a pair of red-legs can each incubate separate clutches. However, there is no evidence of natural immigration from the Continent.

The populations of both species of partridge can be helped by the creation of conservation headlands around fields - strips of ground which are left to seed naturally and are unsprayed, and by the creation of raised earth banks sown with grasses, known as beetle banks. An added bonus is that both these measures also help other ground-nesting birds.

Delightful afternoon at coastal beauty spot

August 1999

One day last week my wife and I spent the afternoon at Burnham Overy Staithe. It was one of those unforgettable days when the sun shone down from an azure sky and yet we were kept pleasantly cool by a gentle easterly breeze.

As we walked along the track towards the dunes, meadow browns, gatekeepers and wall brown butterflies danced ahead of us, while young whitethroats betrayed their presence in the hedgerows by their constant chatter. The air was filled with the smell of fresh pineapples, arising from the pineapple mayweed growing in profusion on the path under our feet. Further along, we found another aromatic plant, the fennel displaying its vibrant yellow florets. The strong smell of aniseed being readily detected on squeezing the stems.

Feeding amongst a herd of grazing cattle was a pair of oystercatchers or "sea pies", which with the sad decline of the snipe and lapwing, may one day become the commonest inland breeding wader in Norfolk. The whispering reeds along the reed-filled dykes no longer held singing reed and sedge warblers, some of which may already have begun their long journey south to wintering areas in West Africa; while the saltings to the west displayed their purple mantle of sea lavender.

As we reached the sand dunes, the vegetation changed and was dominated by marram grass, which holds together the fragile dune system. Here grayling butter-flies were flitting rapidly from hollow to hollow, becoming almost invisible after landing, as they settled parallel with the sun's rays, thus casting virtually no shadow. We crossed the golden sands extending for several miles in both directions, marvel-ling at the few people sharing this idyllic area with us, despite it being mid-summer. How lucky we are to live in Norfolk!

The tide was well out and it was still a fair walk to the edge of the sea, where gulls and terns were feeding in the shallows left by the receding tide. One of the many common gulls had caught a sand eel and was being harried relentlessly by several other birds. Even an attack by a common tern was sufficiently aggressive to cause the bigger bird to drop the eel. It was quickly retrieved but soon lost to a rival gull, which in turn dropped it while juggling with it in the air. Eventually one bird managed to evade its pursuers and land on the beach, whereupon it manoeuvred the sand eel into a headfirst position and quickly swallowed it down.

With the sun twinkling on the rippling water in Burnham harbour, we began to wend our way back to the dunes, having spent a delightful afternoon at one of Norfolk's many coastal gems.

More to a dunnock than meets the eye

January 2001
There's a lot more to the gentle dunnock than meets the eye. For a start, unlike most birds it's got three well-known English names, as well as a whole host of colloquial ones. The word dunnock refers to the grey-brown or "dunn" coloured plumage, while one of the alternatives, hedge sparrow, is from an Old English word which literally translated means "hedge flutterer". The same Icelandic word for flutterer "sporr" was also used for house sparrow, thus these two quite unrelated birds came to be given the same name of sparrow! The third name is hedge accentor, an anglicised version of the original scientific name of the genus, first used by Linnaeus. Literally translated it means "one who sings with another".

The very distinct shuffling gait of a dunnock, combined with the delicate fluttering of the wings used as a display, account for the name of "shufflewing". Although I have been unable to trace a local Norfolk name for the species, in Suffolk it was known as "hedge scrubber".

The eggs of a dunnock are a beautiful pure blue colour and although the nests are often parasitised by cuckoos, the egg of the cuckoo never resembles that of the dunnock, whereas it often does with other host species. This has led to two other amusing names - "foolish sparrow" and "blind dunnock".

To watch a dunnock creeping around a lawn, quickly retreating into cover at the first sign of danger, leads one to believe that it might even be afraid of its own shadow. Actually, this may not be far from the truth. A letter, published in the journal British Birds in 1996, described how a dunnock sprang back from a shallow pool after pecking at the surface of the water, apparently afraid of its own reflection!

While true pair bonds do exist for many dunnocks during the breeding season, other arrangements are not unknown. One of the commonest alternatives involves a polyandrous trio of birds, in which one female is attended by two males. This usually occurs where a female frequents the adjoining territories of two males and these two territories then coalesce. In this situation one of the males, usually the older of the two, becomes dominant, although they may both use the same perches for singing. This is no doubt how the name accentor, mentioned above, arose.

Although the vast majority of British dunnocks are resident, some birds do get very excited in autumn, calling loudly and flying up to the tops of tall bushes, as if they are preparing to migrate.

Whispering reeds - the true sound of Broadland

September 2000

Although I have a small boat of my own, sometimes it's nice to be really lazy and hire one on the Broads, to avoid the hassle of getting it ready, towing it to a launching staithe and cleaning it afterwards. But perhaps that's because I'm not a true boating fanatic.

So it was that in mid-August, Fran and I, and our two nieces, Sarah and Ellie, spent a most enjoyable afternoon on the eastern Broads and their adjoining rivers and dykes. After collecting our day launch from Ken Shepherd, manager of Whispering Reeds Boats at Hickling, we started across the Broad, where I was half-expecting to find navigation a problem due to the presence of stoneworts. But no, despite the water looking clean and healthy, there wasn't a stonewort in sight. Nature has a fascinating way of dealing with potential problems!

Leaving the main Broad along Heigham Sound, we were soon into one of those peaceful stretches for which the Broads are famous (Plate 4). There is an almost timeless quality about these narrow serpentine, waterways, separated from the surrounding grazing marshes by their borders of tall reeds. I half-expected the Edwardian naturalist Miss Emma Turner to appear in her boat around one of the bends!

Although the reedy fringes were fairly quiet, as far as birds were concerned, occasional reed warblers shot across the water in front of us, while delicate common blue damselflies skimmed the surface and the much larger brown hawker dragonflies, with their golden-tinted wings, patrolled their territories above the reeds. Several marsh harriers graced the skies, evidence of the welcome return to former numbers; a greenshank, presumably startled by a passing boat, flew noisily away over our heads and a little gull, half the size of the nearby black-heads, fed tern-like from the surface of a more open stretch of water.

The broken sails of an old windmill made a perfect roosting site for three cormorants, while in the distance the stark outlines of the Martham wind turbines brought us smartly back into the twenty-first century. In a world dominated by cars, phones and a hectic pace of life, surely there is no better way to unwind, than in the tranquillity of Broadland.

Unfortunately, the recent adverse publicity in a national holiday journal has certainly done no good as far as visitor numbers to the Broads are concerned, and this has been compounded by the poor weather this year.

Let's hope we get an "Indian summer", and that visitors will once again discover the delights of Broadland.

Swirling swifts are so hard to count

August 2000
Up until two weeks or so ago, the skies above our garden were alive with the sound of screaming swifts, as they cut through the air on their scimitar-shaped wings. Although it was not easy to follow them, it did seem that some were flying in pairs, while others were clearly in tight-knit family groups. It was even more difficult to count them, as they twisted this way and that, revelling in their mastery of the air, but I did get the impression that there is still a healthy population in and around Sheringham.

Swifts are the fastest of all birds in level flight, with the needle-tailed swift of Asia and Africa having been recorded flying at no less than 105 mph. They are also one of the longest-lived birds for their size. To date, the oldest British-ringed swift was over 16 years, and was estimated to have flown four million miles during its life!

Unlike swallows, swifts are uniformly dark, apart from a pale throat, and for very many years have lived, at least during the summer months, in close association with man. They nest in the roof spaces of older-type properties and as these have been pulled down and replaced with modern housing, fewer suitable nesting sites have been available. Being totally dependent on flying insects as their source of food, adult swifts have to spend many hours each day in pursuit of flies, bugs, hoverflies and even spiders. The latter, although wingless, being carried about in the aerial plankton many hundreds of feet in the air.

This month, hatches of flying ants have been characterised by the swirling mass of swifts and, perhaps surprisingly, vast numbers of black-headed gulls making the most of this feeding bonanza. Unfortunately, many people spray insecticides on the emerging ants and one can only wonder if those that survive are in turn passing the poison on to the birds. Only this summer, I heard of a green woodpecker that was suspected of having died from ingesting ants from a lawn that had been treated with insecticide.

The weather can also have a dramatic effect on available food. In order to cope with cold, wet, windy days when adults are unable to collect sufficient insect prey, nestling swifts enter a state of stupor and can even survive unfed for several days.

Once the adults and young have deserted their breeding sites, they spend all their time on the wing on migration or over their African winter quarters, until returning to nest in Europe the following spring.

Cleaning duty for ants among the feathers

August 2000

I recently wrote about flying ants and their attraction to swifts and black-headed gulls. Certain other species also have an association with ants, but in relationship to feather care, rather than feeding.

Many readers must have seen blackbirds sitting on their lawns or gardens paths, with eyes closed and wings spread, as if in ecstasy. These birds are engaged in passive anting, during which ants are allowed to run up from the ground and through their plumage. The jay is another species, which enjoys this form of activity. Other birds, such as the starling, take a more active role and pick up one or more ants in their bill and apply them to their feathers, particularly to the undersides of the primaries. This is known as active anting.

But why do they do this? It is now generally believed that by choosing ants in which the sting is produced in the form of a spray, a fine jet of formic acid is released from the tip of the ant's abdomen and onto the bird's feathers. This formic acid kills feather parasites such as mites, ticks and lice, and perhaps also helps to remove dirt and dried skin. Having ejected their poison, the bird may then eat the ants, after they have performed their cleaning duty!

Another form of behaviour can easily be mistaken for anting, and this is sunning. Many birds clearly enjoy sunbathing, in just the same way that we do. It frequently follows, or is part of normal preening, and can be seen by house sparrows sitting on a roof, or warblers perched in the sun on the outer branches of a bush or tree. During this activity the feathers are often ruffled to expose the underlying skin. When it occurs on the ground, the bird will half lay with wings drooped, very much like the position adopted in anting.

I well remember coming across a flock of several hundred fieldfares at Felbrigg in March. Rather than actively feeding, many of the birds were simply relaxing in the warm spring sunshine, sitting on the meadow with wings outspread.

Returning to the swifts, not all insects, however, are beneficial to them. In fact, the bird's only real enemy is a small blood-sucking louse-fly *Crataerina pallida*. It's about a centimetre long and having only vestigial wings, spends its life running through the feathers of the swift and feeding on the bird's blood. As ringers of swifts can testify, the insects are not averse to transferring their attentions to man!

Felbrigg Park - a personal favourite

September 1999

Felbrigg Park, the National Trust property in North Norfolk, is worth a visit at any time of the year (Plate 1). Of all the places I go to regularly, it is one of my favourites, and I rarely come away without having seen something of interest.

The estate was the home of Robert Wyndham Ketton-Cremer, one of Norfolk's greatest men of letters, and it was bequeathed to the National Trust on his death in 1969. The land, which was first opened to the public in 1971, includes a rich mosaic of habitats, from open parkland and mature woodland, to mixed farmland, water meadows and a lake.

A recent walk at Felbrigg was on one of those unusual days in Norfolk, when hardly a breath of wind swayed even the smallest of branches; and the mirror-like lake ahead had barely a ripple on its surface (Plate 7). High in the sky, swifts betrayed their presence by their screaming calls, while below them house martins with their gleaming white underparts were feeding on the flying insects rising in the early morning sun. The woods were typically fairly quiet at this time of year, the period during which adult birds are undergoing their annual feather moult. There was only the occasional wren giving its sudden loud burst of song and, in the distance, the raucous cry of a jay.

Felbrigg is one of the best places in the county to see all three species of woodpecker and as I walked across the parkland a green woodpecker could be heard "yaffling", that very distinct, rather haunting call so characteristic of larger areas of woodland.

Woodland edges and rides are often the best places to stand and watch for wildlife; this morning was no exception. The scattered trees at the northern end of the lake were alive with birds. Mixed groups of tits were searching the leaves of the oak trees for insects. As is so often the case, they were accompanied by a treecreeper, which was crawling along the underside of a branch, looking for all the world like a little mouse. As it jerkily moved along, it was probing the crevices of the bark with its decurved bill for any tiny morsels.

I was particularly pleased to see three or four spotted flycatchers in the same area, making frequent aerial sallies out from the branches. Unfortunately, this is a species that has become far scarcer in recent years, and I wondered whether this was a family party of locally-bred birds or migrants passing through on their way south to their African wintering grounds.

Speckled wood is always a fine sight

September 1999

Despite seeing fewer butterflies than usual this summer, the speckled wood made its first ever appearance in our garden in Sheringham. It was many years ago that I saw my first in Devon, ever since when I have always considered it to be one of the most attractive of the woodland butterflies. Its dark brown wings, flecked with creamy spots, mirror the dappled shade in which it's found in glades and along woodland rides. Characteristically it patrols its territory, flying rather weakly and erratically, perching frequently with wings outspread, when its colouration and markings can be seen to provide excellent camouflage.

During the last 200 years, the speckled wood has undergone some dramatic changes in its distribution. In the early nineteenth century it could be found throughout much of the British Isles, whereas 100 years later it was confined mainly to the West Country. Indeed, it was not until the late 1950s that it became wide-spread in Breckland, the only locality in East Anglia where it was anything like common. Since the mid-1980s, small, but well-established colonies have appeared at scattered sites throughout Norfolk.

I first encountered it in North Norfolk in autumn 1992, when one flew across some rough land behind the shingle bank at Weybourne, a most unlikely setting for a woodland species. Two years later, a small colony was located in the trees around Muckleburgh Hill at Weybourne, where they are now a regular sight in summer. The species has two overlapping broods each year, and is on the wing throughout the summer and in the autumn as late as mid-October. Of particular interest is the fact that the speckled wood is unique amongst British butterflies in being able to over-winter as either a chrysalis or a caterpillar, with the latter emerging as an adult about a month later.

Since the Rev F O Morris first produced his illustrated classic A History of British Butterflies in the middle of the nineteenth century, good identification guides have been available for this fascinating group of insects, which are ideal subjects for intro-ducing children to the wonders of nature. As Charles Waterton said in 1871 in his Essays of a Naturalist:

Oh! pleasant, pleasant were the days,
The time when, in our childish plays,
My sister Emmeline and I
Together chased the butterfly!

Woodpecker a welcome visitor to our gardens

October 1999

At a time when we hear a good deal about declines in once common Norfolk birds, it is encouraging to be able to write about one species that has increased in recent years - the great spotted woodpecker (Plate 5). It has always been the most widespread and most numerous of the three woodpecker species in Norfolk, despite its attractive plumage making it a great favourite with the Victorian collectors and taxidermists.

One reason for the recent increase would appear to have been the spread of Dutch elm disease, which resulted in an abundance of loose bark behind which invertebrate prey could more easily be found. The dead and dying trees also provided a plethora of suitable potential nesting sites. At about the same time, great spotted woodpeckers began to become more frequent visitors to both rural and suburban gardens, exploiting the readily available supply of peanuts and fat. As diseased elms have fallen or been removed, this artificial food source has become even more important.

Unfortunately, the lesser spotted woodpecker, the smaller cousin of the more familiar great spotted, remains a rare visitor to bird tables and peanut feeders. Although there was a temporary increase in its numbers with Dutch elm disease, it has once more become an uncommon bird in Norfolk.

However, it's not only peanuts and fat that great spotted woodpeckers find to feed on in gardens. At a recent talk I gave to the Broadland Group of the Norfolk Wildlife Trust, two members of the audience reported them feeding on the flowering spikes of red hot pokers.

Although insects are the main naturally-occurring food of great spotted woodpeckers, conifer seeds are important in winter, particularly in northern Europe. Sheila Basham, an EDP reader from Watton, writing in a letter to the editor, described how a woodpecker, which she correctly believed to be a great spotted, was extracting hazel-nuts from their shells after wedging them in holes in a wooden electricity pole.

In fact, this is one of the few species of woodpecker to use a "tool" as an aid to feeding. The bird may either use an existing crevice in the bark of a tree or else will deliberately drill out a suitably sized hole to hold the nut. Incidentally, the hole or crevice is known as an "anvil", and the same ones may be used over a long period of time, as was the case with that described by Sheila Basham.

As autumn leaves fall

White-winged black tern admired by many

August 2001
When I was phoned two weeks ago about an adult white-winged black tern at Kelling Water Meadows, I dropped everything and drove straight there. Although I had seen many summer-plumaged birds abroad, I had only seen two autumn immatures in Norfolk, and so I knew that this was a bird not to be missed. And what a treat it was! Flying around low over the still water, it frequently dipped down to delicately pick off insects from the surface.

Its close relative, the black tern, is an annual visitor to this area of fresh water at Kelling, albeit in small numbers and usually in spring, but this was the first time that a white-winged black tern had been reported there. In breeding plumage, there is no mistaking the two birds; the silvery-white upperwings contrasting with the dark head and body, as the name white-winged black tern suggests, as compared with the more uniform dark grey wings of the black tern. As it flew past less than 30 yards away, it was also possible to appreciate the slightly broader wings and shorter bill than in a black tern.

Accompanying the tern, and feeding in a very similar manner, was a first-summer little gull, a regular mid-summer visitor to many of the wetland reserves along the North Norfolk coast.

Although the tern was the main attraction, there were plenty of other birds to watch, including a brood of gadwall, only the second year that the species has nested at Kelling Water Meadows. Suddenly, the black-headed gulls that breed on the island took to the air, and the swallows and martins noisily proclaimed the presence of a raptor. Sure enough, an immature marsh harrier drifted across the fields but showed no interest in the wealth of birds on or over the open water.

All this while, a quail had been monotonously giving its distinctive "wet-my-lips" call from the depths of a ripe cereal field; at one moment seeming to be only a short distance away, at the next in the middle of the field. Such is the ventriloquial skill of this diminutive partridge-like bird.

Over the few days that the white-winged black tern was present, it must have been seen by hundreds of observers, thanks to the news being made available by Birdline East Anglia, which is run by Dave Holman and Robin Chittenden in Norwich.

When do birds first learn to sing?

August 2001
In many ways July is one of the quietest months for birds - woods tend to be silent and there is often a noticeable reduction in the number of birds visiting our gardens. For this is the time of year when many adult birds undergo their full feather moult, during which they keep very much to themselves. Not all birds, however, are silent or relatively inactive. For instance, a wren has been particularly vociferous in our garden in the last couple of weeks, his loud and full-bodied song carrying for almost a hundred yards. But why should a wren be singing so late in the season?

Certainly during the spring and early summer, the wren is one of the easiest of birds to stimulate into song, a fact that is useful to know when carrying out a census of breeding birds. Make virtually any sort of squeaking or pishing sound (the noise made by birdwatchers, particularly in North America, to attract birds) and any male wrens in the vicinity will start to sing. Incidentally, the Cetti's warbler is another species that will respond in the same way.

Returning to the wrens that are currently in song, they may be birds with second broods, but I wonder if some that we hear in August could also be birds from the earlier broods that are learning to sing? It is known that all song birds learn the appropriate song at a comparatively early age, rather than simply inheriting the information from their parents. There is a "sensitive" period up to the age of about three months, when this learning process is at its peak. Thus there is no reason why birds fledged early in the breeding season, should not be capable of song by late summer.

This fact was brought home to me several years ago when I was ringing at Weybourne. A young wren that I had ringed in June that year, only a week or so after it had left the nest, was retrapped again in August, by which time it was less than three months old. On being released it perched on top of a nearby bush and burst into song, much to my surprise.

Having thus learnt the basic song, which is stored in the bird's memory, it is further refined and added to by hearing other birds of the same species singing the next spring. This second "sensitive" period up to the age of about nine months is generally the final chance that most birds have to alter or otherwise improve their repertoire.

Whitethroat gets ready for journey to Africa

September 1999

While sitting by my study window last week, I noticed movement in the crab apple tree. Closer inspection through the binoculars revealed it to be one of our locally-bred young robins. I have been watching this particular bird over the last few weeks as it has changed from its scaly juvenile plumage to its more familiar orange-breasted adult attire. On this occasion I discovered that it was chasing a young whitethroat that was busily searching the underside of the leaves for caterpillars and other small items of insect prey. Nearby were feeding both great and blue tits, as well as chaffinches. I began to wonder why the robin had decided to chase the whitethroat, while ignoring the other species. Clearly the robin recognised it as a competitor for food, whereas it did not look upon the other more familiar species in the garden as rivals.

The whitethroat is one of the commonest and most widespread breeding warblers in Norfolk and, in common with the majority of the other members of this family, winters in Africa. Again, like the other warblers, its main items of food consist of insects, although a subtle change in its diet and eating habits occurs in late summer and early autumn.

As a result of hormonal influences, the bird's appetite increases considerably and in addition to feeding upon insects, it starts to feed on fruits and berries, which are rich in carbohydrate. This leads to deposits of fat being laid down under the skin, which can be utilised later during the bird's long flight to its wintering grounds, which, in the case of the whitethroat, are in West Africa. In addition to the fat, the flight muscles increase in size, again in preparation for migration. During this period of fattening, a bird's weight can almost double simply by this deposition of fat and the increase in muscle bulk.

Once the optimum weight for migration has been reached, which again is under hormonal control, the bird will bide its time until suitable weather conditions for migration occur. On the afternoon of departure, it will rest rather than feed, and under cover of darkness will begin its journey south. In the case of a whitethroat this will consist of short flights of about 50 miles each night. By migrating at night the whitethroat can avoid the attention of any predators and is able to use the daylight hours, not only to rest, but also to take on additional food, which will be converted into fat for the continuation of its journey.

Bill size and shape adapted to lifestyle

August 2000

In an earlier article I have mentioned the specially adapted bill of the nightjar, which enables it to trap moths and other flying insects in flight. The swift, another aerial feeder, also has a similar bill shape and wide gape for the same purpose. In all species of birds, the type of food normally taken dictates both bill length and shape. Faced with an unfamiliar bird, it is always worth taking note of the bill as this should at least enable it to be placed in its correct family.

The broad, triangular-shaped bills of finches will be familiar to most readers. These are designed to allow the birds to remove the hard, outer case of a nut and reach the kernel inside. This design is taken to the extreme in the hawfinch, which has a massively heavy bill for the size of the bird, so powerful that even cherry stones can be cracked open. At the other extreme, the narrower more pointed bill of a goldfinch allows it to extract seeds from the heads of teasels. This plant is so named, because the dried prickly heads were at one time used to "tease out" or raise the nap on woven cloth.

While the bills of crossbills are specially shaped to allow the birds to extract seeds from cones, even these vary according to the type of tree on which they generally feed. The slighter bill of the two-barred crossbill is adapted for larch cones and the stouter bill of the parrot crossbill for tackling the larger cones of the Scot's pine.

The bills of many insectivorous birds, such as the willow warbler, are thin and pointed enabling them to delicately pick up spiders and small non-flying insects. Then there are those species which feed predominantly by waiting on an exposed branch, from where they make forages to catch insects on the wing, such as the spotted flycatcher. In these, the bill is pointed but much broader at the base, thus increasing the catching area.

Between these two extremes of a broad, finch-like bill and a fine, insectivorous one, is that possessed by the non-specialist feeders. These birds take a wide variety of food items from berries and other fruit to worms and insects, such as leatherjackets. Many of our familiar garden birds fall into this category - for instance starling and blackbird. It is also, of course, these omnivorous species that readily take unnatural food that we put out, such as bread.

East wind promised a "fall" of migrants

August 2001

Mid-August and the promise of an easterly wind with rain approaching from the west, what more could a birdwatcher want? Or at least, so it seemed a couple of weekends ago.

Dawn found me at my ringing site at Weybourne with an air of excitement and expectation (and Fran, my wife, thought that I was just there for the birds, she'd never even heard of Dawn!). A few skittish song thrushes noisily left the bushes as I approached, almost certainly the vanguard of those that arrive in early autumn from the Continent. The robins that were ticking from deep inside the cover were probably local birds; as were the rather fluffy, young whitethroats that anxiously churred as I went round setting up my nets. The thin "tsweep" of a yellow wagtail as it flew west was an encouraging sign that some migrants were on the move but as time passed it was apparent that the expected "fall" of birds had not materialised.

While it is true that the heaviest passage of visible migrants, such as swallows, martins, wagtails and pipits usually occurs during the first few hours after dawn, some of the most exciting "falls" of warblers, flycatchers and redstarts that I have witnessed have been in mid-morning or even early afternoon. So maybe all was not yet lost.

Despite the lack of migrants, there was still plenty to keep me occupied. The small water-filled scrape behind the beach had, once again, provided a breeding site for a pair of dabchicks or little grebes. The three surviving young, out of the original brood of five, had divided themselves between the two adults. Their constant peeping calls, although providing an attractive auditory backdrop, must have nearly driven their parents to distraction, so persistent were they in their demand for food. By now over a week old, they were still little more than balls of black feathers with a few pale stripes on the head and neck.

At sea, a few gannets were flying south, a mixture of adult and juvenile birds, while close inshore some of the local common and Sandwich terns were busily fishing, not yet ready to begin their journey southwards to their wintering areas in West Africa. The distinctive flight call of a green sandpiper overhead made me look up, and in so doing I noticed a hobby that was chasing a hapless young house martin. For over a minute they twisted and turned in deadly pursuit, until surprisingly the martin escaped, shaken but otherwise unharmed.

No "fall" did occur that day, but did it matter?

Delightful bird always a pleasure to behold

August 2001

My love affair with pied flycatchers began over 40 years ago during my first visit to Norfolk. A school friend and I came up to Cley, in his old banger, and we camped between the Beach Road and the West Bank for a week in early September. In those days, the late 1950s and early 1960s, the first part of September was the time to visit Cley - east winds could almost be guaranteed, bringing with them those drift migrants that we all dreamt of seeing.

Our first full day saw us walking out to Blakeney Point, but apart from a handful of willow warblers, there was very little to find in either the *Suaeda* bushes or the plantation on the Point. A little disappointed, we visited Salthouse Heath in late afternoon, and there to our great delight we found two pied flycatchers in some stunted roadside trees on the seaward side of the heath; the first that we had ever seen. Slightly smaller than spotted flycatchers, with which we were familiar, and with pale, unmarked underparts and a distinct white wing flash, we were enchanted by their rather nervous habit of frequently cocking their tail and flicking one wing upwards.

To non-birdwatchers, autumn pied flycatchers may appear to be boring little birds; they might even be classified as "LBJs" or "Little Brown Jobs", but to us on that day they were absolute magic. Since that first sighting, I must have seen hundreds more, but their attraction has not diminished one iota.

As summer visitors to Europe from their sub-Saharan wintering grounds, they breed mainly in the north and west of Britain, and it is as autumn migrants that they occur most frequently in East Anglia. Despite this, small numbers are seen each spring, when the males are in their distinct black-and-white breeding plumage, from which the species gets its name. One such male that I ringed at Sheringham in May 1981 was retrapped at a nest box in Cumbria four summers later, indicating that, at least, some of our spring birds are of British breeding stock.

In the autumn, however, pied flycatchers are one of the most characteristic species involved in "falls" of Scandinavian drift migrants, even if numbers have tended to be smaller in recent years. While the majority of pied flycatchers are seen at coastal locations, occasional birds are recorded inland. I well remember looking out of the window of my Hampstead flat, while I was a student in London, and seeing a pied flycatcher in the garden, another unforgettable sighting of this delightful species.

An exciting time ahead for birders

September 1999

To many birdwatchers the excitement of autumn birding is unparalleled. Not only is there the possibility of seeing a rare bird, but also the opportunity to witness the annual comings and goings of our summer and winter visitors. Everyone interested in the countryside is aware that birds such as swallows, whitethroats and spotted fly-catchers are summer migrants to Norfolk, while fieldfares and redwings are here during the winter months. However, there are also a large number of birds that simply visit Norfolk as passage migrants, and some of the species involved will probably come as a surprise to many readers.

Take, for example, the dunnock or hedge sparrow, familiar to many people as the small, greyish-brown bird that shuffles around our lawns, often keeping near to the safety of the cover provided by the herbaceous border. Its timid nature makes it look as if it would be afraid of its own shadow. In autumn, small parties of dunnocks may be seen flitting excitedly around the tops of bushes and low trees along the coast, calling repeatedly, before flying off together. These are likely to be our local birds.

But dunnocks in Scandinavia are migratory and birds from this population almost certainly pass through the county each autumn. Last October, for instance, one that I caught at Weybourne had already been ringed in southern Sweden, only two weeks previously. This was the first Swedish-ringed dunnock to be found in the British Isles, although others ringed elsewhere in Europe have been recovered here.

Returning to this autumn, a brief spell of easterly winds towards the end of August produced a small "fall" of migrants along the Norfolk coast. At Weybourne, amongst the willow and garden warblers, were a few redstarts, with their quivering chestnut tails. The young males just showing a suggestion of the striking head pattern, which they will have acquired when they return to breed in Europe next spring. Also involved in this movement were a few pied flycatchers, one even reaching as far inland as Eaton Rise in Norwich. Jean Clissold who takes part in the BTO Garden BirdWatch, sadly found one dead under her kitchen window; the first record of the species in her garden.

My most exciting find, so far this autumn, has been a barred warbler present for just one day at Weybourne in mid-August. As the name implies, adult barred warblers are indeed barred; but all those that we see in autumn are juveniles and as such are rather plain grey-brown, not dissimilar in appearance to a large, longer-tailed version of a garden warbler. The species breeds in central and eastern Europe but is a regular, if scarce, autumn migrant to the British east coast.

Pleasures of seawatching in the teeth of a gale

August 2001

While holidaymakers occupy the seafront shelters at Sheringham during the summer, by the time that autumn comes the shelters are often taken over by seawatching enthusiasts, and seats are at a premium.

When I first moved to this delightful North Norfolk seaside town in 1972, a mere handful of local birdwatchers could be found gazing intently seawards during the autumn, watching the offshore passage of birds. But how things have changed! Amongst the stalwarts of those early days were the late Jim Marsham, with his enormous pair of 20x binoculars, and a young teenager, Kevin Shepherd, who was to become one of the county's top birders, and certainly Norfolk's most enthusiastic seawatcher.

It really does take something very special to sit from dawn till dusk, on a hard bench, with a strong northerly gale gusting straight towards you. Squally showers often add to the discomfort, but frequently that is the reality of seawatching. Of course, conditions aren't always that bad - often they're even worse! Especially in late October and November when the wind chill factor lowers the temperature to well below freezing. So why on earth do so many birdwatchers do it?

Certainly in recent years, seawatching has become an increasingly popular part of the birding scene. Take virtually any headland around the coast of England, and given a strong onshore wind, it can be guaranteed that binoculars and telescopes will be trained on the horizon. For those of us living in East Anglia, the attraction is almost certainly our only opportunity of watching seabirds that breed on offshore islands, often many hundreds, if not thousands, of miles away - birds such as gannets, shearwaters and skuas. Of course, there is also the pleasure of witnessing the arrival of ducks and waders that will be spending the winter months with us, and the departure of some species, such as the terns, which are heading south to their African wintering areas.

Seabirds, in particular, are great travellers and one of the undoubted attractions of seawatching is the chance of seeing some unusual or, occasionally, very rare species. The main problem, however, is that each bird is normally visible for less than a minute as it flies through your field of view. Given the difficulty of picking up a bird, over the vast expanse of empty sea, you're actually lucky if you see it for that long, but despite this, seawatching can be very rewarding (and enjoyable!).

Plate 1   *Previous page* A crisp winter's morning in Felbrigg woods
Plate 2   *Top* A handsome cock wheatear in spring plumage, caught for ringing
              Bottom A female dotterel en route to its mountain-top breeding site

Plate 3   *Top* The song thrush, no longer a common garden bird
Bottom A nestling starling awaits the return of its parents

Plate 4   *Top* A freshly emerged broad-bodied chaser
             Bottom A young great crested grebe hitches a ride on its parent's back
Plate 5   *Opposite* A great spotted woodpecker, aged as a juvenile by its red crown

Plate 6   *Top* Looking east from Weybourne during an autumn gale
Bottom A fulmar on its breeding ledge on Sheringham cliffs

Plate 7 *Top* A pair of Canada geese, a characteristic bird of parkland lakes
Bottom Little egrets are now a common sight around the East Anglian coast

Plate 8   *Top* A long-eared owl's "ear" tufts are used as a warning signal
Bottom The extensive reed-beds at Walberswick

Plate 9 *Top* The first-winter ivory gull on the beach at Aldeburgh
Bottom The attractive underwing pattern of a common blue

Plate 10 *Top* A golden plover in winter plumage, the underparts are black in summer
Bottom A juvenile red-backed shrike, or butcher bird, is caught for ringing

Plate 11 *Top* The toes of the grey phalarope are partially lobed as an aid to swimming
Bottom Steller's jay, a characteristic bird of the west coast forests of Canada

Plate 12 *Top* The killdeer is one of the most widespread waders in North America
Bottom A rufous-tailed jacamar poses by the roadside in Tobago

Plate 13 *Top* An incubating female white-necked jacobin, rarely photographed at the nest
Bottom Montezuma oropendolas nest in large tree-top colonies

Plate 14   *Top* Mizen Head, one of the best places to see choughs in south-west Ireland
                 Bottom Owl's eye butterfly, an inhabitant of the rain forest
Plate 15   *Opposite* A young spectacled owl at Sacha Lodge in Ecuador

Plate 16 *Top* The white-throated toucan uses its long bill to reach fruit at the end of branches
Bottom Autumn sunset over Lake Erie, Canada

Incredible homing instincts of shearwaters

September 2001

Early September often proves to be the most rewarding time for seawatching and this year has proved to be no exception. North-westerly winds at the end of August were somewhat disappointing, as far as good numbers of seabirds were concerned. However, I was fortunate enough to arrive in the seafront shelters at Sheringham, late one afternoon, just as a Cory's shearwater flew lazily east. With only about 80 previous Norfolk records, this is one of the less common species of shearwater around the East Anglian coast and it is also the largest to visit British waters.

The forecast of a strong northerly wind a few days later ensured that I arrived at my seawatching site at Weybourne shortly after dawn (Plate 6). Almost the first bird I saw on this occasion was a sooty shearwater, a uniformly dark bird that sheared through the wave troughs, dipping from side to side, its wing tips just skimming the turbulent sea. During the course of the morning many more were to pass, some no more than a couple of hundred yards offshore. Sooty shearwaters are transequatorial migrants, the nearest breeding colonies to the British Isles being in the Falkland Isles, demonstrating the vast distances travelled by many seabirds. In common with most other species of shearwater, they nest colonially in burrows on islands, and as such are very vulnerable to any ground predators that may be accidentally or intentionally introduced to the islands, such as the brown rat.

Several small groups of Manx shearwaters were also seen on the same morning. These are the most frequently seen member of the family off East Anglia with sightings from mid-June onwards. The breeding colonies on the islands off the western coasts of Britain and Ireland hold a major proportion of the world population. Like the sooty shearwaters, they too are transequatorial migrants, departing their island colonies in the autumn, to begin their long ocean journey to winter off the eastern coast of South America. During their ocean crossing, the westerly winds of the roaring forties have even pushed a few around to the other side of the world; one ringed on a Welsh island being found in Australia!

Although Manx shearwaters so far off course are unlikely to return home again, they do possess an amazing ability to reorientate. A breeding adult, that had been previously ringed, was transported to Boston, Massachusetts, and was found back in its breeding burrow on a Welsh island just twelve and a half days later!

Life is a struggle for albino birds

February 2000

A couple of weeks ago, Daphne ffisk rang to say that she had seen a completely white pheasant in her garden at Bramerton. Although she regularly has a few pheasants visiting her garden, which backs on to open land, this was the first occasion on which she had ever seen an albino one. Albinism, in fact, is not that uncommon in pheasants, and I have seen several over the years in North Norfolk. A count of 22 white pheasants at Winterton in September 1995, however, was most unusual.

This abnormal plumage, due to a complete loss of pigment in the feathers, has been recorded in a large number of bird species, as well as in many other animal groups. There are several disadvantages in being albino, as far as birds are concerned. Firstly, the lack of pigment weakens the feather structure and the feathers wear more rapidly. For this reason many species of gull, which are naturally white or pale grey, have black wing tips to reduce excessive abrasion. Weakening of the flight feathers in albino birds may also make them less mobile.

Secondly, the loss of pigment also occurs in the retina, at the back of eye, resulting in the characteristic pink eyes of albinos. This, in turn, produces impaired vision in bright light. Finally, albino birds tend to be short-lived as they are more conspicuous and therefore more liable to predation. A bird of prey, for instance, is far more likely to take an individual from a flock if it is different from the rest. Albino birds therefore miss out on all counts - they are white, may be less mobile and in bright conditions may be less able to see danger approaching.

A letter in the September issue of the journal British Birds, suggests that albinism may actually be commoner in birds than observations suggest, as most are taken by predators in the first few weeks after fledging. Total albinism is usually inherited as a recessive gene, suggesting that the large number of white pheasants recorded at Winterton in autumn 1995, were the offspring of a pair both carrying the responsible gene. However, partial albinism, in which individual feathers or groups of feathers are white, is much commoner, and the area involved may increase after successive moults.

Always plenty to see from coastal footpath

November 1999

A walk along the cliff-top path between Sheringham and Weybourne can almost always guarantee two things. Firstly it will be windy and secondly some birds of interest will be seen, irrespective of the time of year.

Looking north from the coastal footpath, the vast, grey expanse of the North Sea was very obvious recently, as I walked eastwards from the beach car park at Weybourne. Small groups of cormorants flew from the direction of Cley, to fish off-shore or loaf around on the groynes at Sheringham, characteristically with their wings outspread. It was not long before the sleek, graceful lines of a pale phase adult arctic skua appeared flying close inshore over the breakers. I never tire of watching these pirates of the avian world and it was soon involved in an aerial pursuit with a Sandwich tern. Twisting and turning, it did not give up the chase until the tern had disgorged some partly digested food which the skua adeptly caught in mid-air.

Further out, about 50 great black-backed gulls were wheeling around the stern of a crab boat. The crew of two were hauling the pots, as the boat slowly drifted along, and as the pots were emptied the gulls squabbled over the discarded contents. However, this was a mere fraction of the numbers of this gull that used to be recorded off the Norfolk coast during the late nineteenth and early twentieth centuries. Then their presence used to coincide with the herring fishing season, between late August and early December.

At that time, thousands of great black-backed and smaller numbers of herring gulls, daily followed the herring drifters to the herring grounds in the North Sea, to return to their resting places, later in the day. On occasions the movements were on a mammoth scale. In 1913, Bernard Riviere recorded an astonishing total of 72,000 large gulls, 80% of which were adult great black-backs, moving north-west off Sea Palling on a single day in October. This passage coincided with the season's record herring catches made by Yarmouth boats at the time.

Turning my attention to the landward side of the cliffs, I was pleased to see the wide strip of set-aside by the coastal path, where clovers, vetches and plantains were growing in profusion. Such areas are so important for ground-feeding birds such as skylarks, meadow pipits and linnets. While the presence of one or two corn buntings here this summer was almost certainly related to this old fashioned type of habitat.

Looking for fulmars on their cliff ledges

August 1999

The fulmar should be a familiar bird to anyone walking along or below the cliffs between Weybourne and Cromer. Superficially resembling a gull, the fulmar is in fact a "tubenose", a group that includes the shearwaters and petrels. The strange swelling above the base of the bill, from which the group gets its name, is associated with an enlargement of the part of the brain concerned with the sense of smell. Fulmars and other "tubenoses" almost certainly locate their food and breeding site, as well as other fulmars, by this sense of smell.

Just under 60 years ago, in 1940, fulmars were first recorded "prospecting", as potential nesting sites, the boulder clay cliffs at Weybourne. As a result of this activity, the well-known Norfolk ornithologist Dick Bagnall-Oakeley, who was a school master at Gresham's School, Holt, cut out some artificial ledges with the help of some of his pupils lowered on ropes from the top of the cliffs. One of whom, David Sadler, lived to tell the tale and is still an active birder in the same area! Their efforts were rewarded in 1947, when five pairs were present on the man-made ledges and successful breeding was first proved.

Fulmars take several years to reach sexual maturity and are usually between six and twelve years old before first attempting to breed; in addition each pair only produces a single egg annually. Despite these facts, about 50 pairs were present between Weybourne and Cromer within ten years, the number increasing to over 100 pairs at its peak.

Unfortunately in the early 1990s, rats and foxes began to raid the cliff ledges on which the fulmars were breeding, predating both eggs and young. Numbers fell dramatically and by the mid-1990s only three or four young were fledged from this area. Cliff falls during winter storms also resculpture the cliff face, changing the number of available ledges from year to year.

A walk along the beach at Weybourne this summer, revealed only a handful of pairs on the ledges along the first mile or so. While at least one bird was incubating its single white egg (Plate 6), the others may well have been non-breeding pairs - this is always the problem in attempting to decide exactly how many fulmars are nesting each year. One short section of sandy cliff also held a fine colony of sand martins. Judging from the number of apparently occupied burrows, about 200 pairs were present. Sand martin numbers also fluctuate enormously from year to year, but that is a different story for another day.

Spectacular passage of hirundines

October 1999

Last week saw an unprecedented passage of swallows and house martins in East Anglia, although it is never easy estimating bird numbers, especially when they are passing throughout the day on a broad front. However, one observer reported an incredible 60,000 house martins flying west at Overstrand in just over two hours, while many tens of thousands of both swallows and martins were seen flying west all along the North Norfolk coast.

A similar story was unfolding at Landguard Point Bird Observatory, near Felixstowe in Suffolk where huge numbers of hirundines (swallows and martins) were flying south. There was also a constant passage of both swallows and house martins flying west throughout the day over parts of London, so the movement clearly affected a large part of south-east England.

Unlike many of our summer visitors that migrate at night, hirundines are diurnal migrants and so heavy movements, such as occurred last week, are readily seen. The number of birds involved on this occasion, however, was probably unparalleled. In Norfolk, the autumn passage of swallows usually peaks in late August or the first half of September and prior to this year, the largest day-count had been 12,000 swallows west at Sheringham on September 12, 1995.

House martin passage tends to peak later, probably as a result of their more extended breeding season, and heavy autumn movements have been noted in the county since the early part of the twentieth century. Riviere recorded 15,000 flying west at Overstrand on September 13, 1905, while in more recent times 25,000 flew west at Sheringham on the same day as the swallows mentioned above, a day total which was eclipsed at Mundesley, three weeks later, when 33,500 flew east on October 4, 1995. These heavy autumn passages of house martins are really a most spectacular sight, as loose flocks of several hundred noisy birds pass low over one's head, with wave after wave appearing, often for several hours.

The birds involved in such autumn movements are almost certainly of Continental origin, having crossed the North Sea from the Low Countries or possibly southern Scandinavia. On reaching East Anglia, they usually follow the coastline in either a southerly or westerly direction, depending on their point of arrival. Last week, though, birds were also reported from many inland localities. In the Brecks, at Thetford, for instance, large numbers of swallows were reported flying south-west, presumably on their way to the English south coast, from where they could continue their journey south to their African wintering grounds.

Safety in numbers at bird roosts

November 1999

Many thanks to all the readers who responded to my request for information on the amazing passage of swallows and house martins that took place in late September and early October. All of the information has been passed on to the county bird recorders and will be incorporated into a future article in the Norfolk Bird Report.

Of particular interest was a long letter from my old friend Alec Bull of East Tuddenham, co-author of the highly acclaimed A Flora of Norfolk, which was published earlier this summer. Not only did Alec report a heavy westerly passage of swallows all the way from Fakenham to King's Lynn on September 27, but also some fascinating details about swallows roosting in a field of maize near Shipdham airfield.

His daughter, Sally Rix, had first observed this phenomenon in autumn 1998 and again for the first time this year on August 30. On that date, an estimated 2000 swallows hawked for insects over the maize until dropping in small groups into the crop to roost. Similar behaviour was noted on several evenings during the next ten days. Interestingly, the field was not used again as a roost until the heavy passage noted by Alec on September 27.

Swallows normally form communal roosts in reed-beds and the use of maize appears to be a recent development. In reed-beds, pied wagtails are often "bed fellows" of the swallows, although they are normally present in far smaller numbers. This was also the case in the maize field at Shipdham, where 30 pied wagtails first arrived to roost in early September. The habit appeared to catch on, for when the maize was cut in early October, well over 100 homeless pied wagtails were left to wonder where the cover had gone.

Of course, the best known pied wagtail roost in Norfolk in the last few years has been in the plane trees in Brigg Street, Norwich. A couple of weeks ago, I spent a fascinating hour watching them arrive and settling in, amidst the bustle of the busy shoppers below. My vantage point was the top floor of the Malthouse multi-storey car park which overlooked that part of the city. Before dusk the wagtails began to gather on the flat roofs of the surrounding buildings, before dropping, in small groups, into the plane trees. There they joined several hundred noisy starlings, already perched in the trees, both species clearly aware that there was safety in numbers.

Autumn arrival of wintering wildfowl

October 2000

Every autumn thousands of wildfowl fly to Britain to overwinter. These include breeding birds from as far afield as Greenland, Iceland, Scandinavia and northern Russia. From September to mid-November, a good selection of these swans, ducks and geese can be seen passing west offshore along the North Norfolk coast.

Although the largest numbers are generally recorded on days with strong onshore, northerly winds, the passage continues unseen throughout the autumn. For like many other birds, wildfowl migrate largely by night, choosing in preference light following winds and cloudless skies. The most numerous are teal and wigeon, and it is not unusual for the two species to migrate together in mixed flocks. Teal, the smallest of the European ducks, feed in shallow water, dabbling and up-ending; wigeon, on the other hand, feed mainly by grazing on coastal mudflats and saltings, as well as on inland fields.

Comparatively few mallard are seen on passage in autumn, although it is known from wildfowl counts that many must arrive during the hours of darkness. The same applies to that most elegant of ducks, the pintail. Drake pintails, their dark brown heads and long necks delicately marked with a fine white streak extending to the nape, are surely one of the most attractive of ducks and certainly one of my favourites. In flight the females are subtly different from the other species and it is always satisfying to recognise them as they fly west in autumn.

As well as freshwater duck, several species of sea duck are also recorded in varying numbers around the East Anglian coast at this time of year. The most numerous are common scoter, arriving from their breeding grounds in Fennoscandia and Russia. Both sexes are uniformly dark, but it is only the adult drakes that are truly black. On occasions, a thousand or more scoters have been counted flying west off the North Norfolk coast during the course of a single day, but smaller numbers are usually involved. During the winter they feed mainly on molluscs, principally the blue mussel, and traditionally the largest winter flocks are located off The Wash and north-west Norfolk. Occasionally, the common scoters are joined by the rarer and larger velvet scoters, easily recognised in flight by the distinct white patch on the rear of the inner half of the upperwing, an area known as the speculum.

In wildfowl, pair bonds are formed during the winter and the drakes tend to return to the ducks' natal areas the following spring. As usual, it's a case of the females leading the males astray!

Another memorable visit to Titchwell

October 2000

The memories from certain days out birding remain with you for a long time, and I'm sure that a visit to the RSPB's Titchwell Reserve, a couple of weeks ago, will be just such an occasion.

It was a pleasantly warm, if overcast autumn day, with a light southerly breeze and as I walked along the track to the first hide, I was greeted by the pinging of a small party of bearded tits flying high above the marsh. Initially it seemed that they were about to depart to the east, but suddenly they plummeted back into the reeds, as if they'd simply changed their minds - typical autumn behaviour after a successful breeding season. Nowadays it's hard to visit Titchwell without seeing a little egret (Plate 7) and sure enough, one was perched in one of the dead trees, bordering the marsh, accompanied by a few cormorants; while off to the west, three more were feeding on the saltmarsh.

As it was high tide, I decided to walk directly out to the beach to see if I could locate the flock of common scoters reported the previous day. With the sun now out, and directly behind us, and only a very slight sea swell, conditions were ideal for picking out any birds that were drifting past. We were soon on to several great crested grebes, as well as a fine red-necked grebe, still in partial breeding plumage. The shorter, darker neck and less elegant lines of the red-necked grebe were clearly visible, as was the yellow on the bill. A little later, a slavonian grebe, was also picked up, although it spent most of its time underwater!

Amongst the red-throated divers swimming offshore, was one still in full summer plumage, showing the deep maroon throat, in addition to a most handsome black-throated diver, with its characteristic dove grey crown and hind neck. Unfortunately, the scoter flock was well out to sea, but eventually a sharp-eyed observer declared that he had managed to pick out the adult drake surf scoter, a very rare trans-Atlantic visitor to Norfolk, which had been seen the previous day. With the eye of faith, I was just able to make out the white patch on its nape, as it bobbed around in the swell.

But the best was yet to come - a most confiding spotted crake creeping around the muddy fringe of the island hide; and I haven't even had a chance to mention the black-necked stilt, pomarine skua and Lapland bunting. There was just so much to see!

This lively little bird is difficult to focus on

December 2002

We have noticed a relative abundance of coal tits in our garden this year and I wonder whether other readers have noted a similar increase. Of course, some readers may be unfamiliar with these delightful little birds. In size they are slightly smaller than blue tits, with a black cap and black throat, and a narrow double white wing bar. But the one feature that distinguishes them from all other species of tits is the white patch on the nape.

Coal tits are widely distributed throughout the British Isles, tending to favour coniferous woodland, at least during the summer months. Along with goldcrests, they are characteristic birds of mature conifer plantations, and indeed, they are often the only two species encountered in this type of habitat. Both species tend to feed at the tops of the trees and on the outer branches, invariably flitting from tree to tree, just as you get them in focus in your binoculars! The bills of coal tits are finer than the other species of tits, enabling them to probe the clusters of pine needles for the larvae of insects and spiders. During autumn and winter they also feed on conifer seeds and beech mast.

Although British coal tits are sedentary, they do tend to wander away from their breeding sites in autumn, and are frequent visitors to garden bird tables. Even here they are not the easiest of birds to study, for having extracted a sunflower seed or peanut from the holder, they invariably fly off to conceal it for later consumption or disappear to eat it out of sight! It is their habit of storing food in the autumn and early winter that enables them to survive periods of severe weather despite their small size.

They are often more vocal than other tits during the winter months, their distinct "sitchu-sitchu-sitchu", appearing to be used both as a song and a contact call. It is always faster and higher pitched than the great tit's familiar "teacher-teacher-teacher", and on occasions can recall the song of a chiffchaff.

Like other members of the family, coal tits nest in holes in trees, but also not infrequently will choose a small cavity in the ground, such as an old mouse hole or under the roots of a fallen tree. Nest boxes are more likely to be selected by coal tits if the opening consists of a narrow slit, that is inaccessible to blue and great tits, and if the box is placed on the trunk of a conifer tree.

Autumn migrants arrive at last

November 1999

As dawn broke and the sky gradually lightened, it was immediately apparent that it was going to be one of those mornings when almost anything could turn up. Despite the forecast of easterly winds, it was surprisingly calm at first, but the constant calls of migrating birds overhead was enough to indicate that this would be a good day. The autumn up to now had been very disappointing, but on this particular morning, our patience was to be rewarded.

For the first two hours after dawn, the sky was filled with the sights and sounds of birds purposefully making their way westwards along the North Norfolk coast. Loose parties of chaffinches and bramblings, giving their characteristic flight calls, flew over, some dropping to rest in the nearby cover of the bushes. Larger, tighter groups of starlings flew silently west. Noisy blackbirds and fieldfares, freshly arrived from the Continent, fed voraciously on the few remaining blackberries. Suddenly, a silent woodcock exploded from under my feet, as I started to wander around checking each bramble patch for migrants. Robins were ticking from the shelter of many of the clumps and the thin calls of goldcrests could be heard in the nearby pines; while offshore hundreds of brent geese streamed west, in long straggly lines.

As I walked through the rough grassland behind the shingle bank at Weybourne, a repeated sparrow-like cheep was instantly recognizable - a Richard's pipit. In size and general colouration like a skylark but with a noticeably longer tail, it hovered over the long grass before flying westwards. Richard's pipit is a Siberian species which was formerly an extreme rarity in Norfolk, but which has become far more frequent since the mid-1960s. Nowadays several are recorded annually each autumn along the coastal strip between Cromer and Cley.

At this point, I was joined by two birding friends from Weybourne, John Wallis and Fred Lambert, but despite much searching, we were unable to relocate the bird. By now it was mid-morning and the early rush of migrants was over, with only a few small parties of meadow pipits still passing west. As we continued to search the bushes, we disturbed a fine short-eared owl that had taken temporary shelter in a stunted hawthorn, while a male black redstart was hawking for insects from a pylon at the weather station. Although several other much rarer birds were seen elsewhere in Norfolk that day, we had at least found these birds ourselves and that to me is the real joy of birdwatching.

An owl is simply a cat with wings

October 2001

Owls have often been described as cats with wings, and in many ways this is true. While hunting they are prepared to wait silently and motionless for long periods before suddenly pouncing on their prey; they possess long, sharp claws; they often hunt at night, and at times they can be incredibly noisy. So what are the special adaptations that enable owls to thrive so successfully in their strange twilight world?

Perhaps the most striking feature of an owl is its large, round, almost human-like face, and it is in the anatomy of the skull that many of its specialised characteristics are found. The majority of owls are nocturnal. Although it is not true that owls can actually see in total darkness, they do have to be able to hunt for their food under conditions of very low light. This is achieved by having comparatively large, forward-facing eyes, which provide excellent binocular vision. The ability to judge distance accurately is largely dependent on being able to focus on an object with both eyes simultaneously. Try closing one eye, yourself, to see just how difficult it is to assess distance under these circumstances. One of the most endearing habits of owls is their head bobbing action, which again is another ploy to help them to judge distance by viewing an object from different angles.

An owl's hearing is also particularly acute, another extremely valuable asset if hunting at night. Birds have no external ears, as such, and in owls the sounds travel through large vertical openings on the sides of the skull to the internal organs of hearing. The openings are concealed by the feathers of the facial discs, behind which are fringes of short, stiff feathers that are carried on flaps that can be moved to scan around for sound. The "ear" tufts found in certain species of owls, in fact, having nothing at all to do with the sense of hearing (Plate 8).

For their size and weight, owls have very broad, and often comparatively long wings, enabling them to fly apparently effortlessly in a characteristically buoyant manner, avoiding the need for frequent flapping. Silent approach to their intended prey is also aided by their generally softer plumage and by the fine comb-like structure to the leading edges of their flight feathers.

Finally, their hawk-like, hooked bills and long, sharp claws are both adaptations to their predatory feeding habits, while their feathered legs and feet provide protection against any bites from their mammalian prey.

Lemmings control influxes of owls

October 2001

I have previously discussed the various anatomical adaptations that have allowed owls to successfully exploit a nocturnal existence. Of the five species that breed in East Anglia, the most numerous and widespread is the tawny owl, and is the one that is most likely to be spotted at its daytime roost. Attention is often drawn to the presence of a roosting tawny owl by the persistent and characteristic calls of black-birds, chaffinches and tits, as they noisily betray its roost site, high up in a tall tree. Once discovered, the owl will usually choose a different site on subsequent days. However, some roosts are used over a period of many months, or even years, such as that frequented in the very tall pine near the monument in Holkham Park.

Tawny owls are most vociferous during the winter months, the loud hooting being used by the birds to indicate their presence to other neighbouring owls. The use of sound is even more important to nocturnal species than it is to song birds, as visual clues to the extent of a bird's territory is next to useless.

Probably most people's favourite is the barn owl, a truly cosmopolitan species that is found on every continent except Antarctica. In recent years, much effort has gone into reversing the downward trend in numbers. As a result, once again it is not an uncommon sight to see one or two hunting at dusk, or even in the middle of the day, over favoured areas, such as the coastal marshes of North Norfolk.

My own favourite, however, is the little owl, a bird it is so easy to overlook despite it being largely diurnal. The species was introduced into Britain in the nineteenth century and had become a common breeding bird by the 1930s. Unfortunately, changing agricultural practices, such as the removal of hedges and trees, has caused a decline in the population since the 1950s. Unlike the other owls in Britain it feeds largely on earthworms and insects, thus the increasing use of insecticides has also had a detrimental effect.

The size of owl populations is very much dependent on the availability of prey and this is particularly well shown by the occasional autumn influxes of large numbers of short-eared owls into East Anglia. The northern European population of these owls increases dramatically in "good" lemming years. In the following year, insufficient food is available for the large number of owls that were successfully raised the previous year. As a result they have to wander further afield to survive and many arrive on the east coast of Britain.

Unique character of Suffolk coastline

November 2001
Earlier this month, Fran and I spent a couple of most enjoyable days in Suffolk. Using Aldeburgh as our base, we explored the stretch of coastline from Benacre in the north to Sizewell in the south.

One of my earliest visits to Suffolk was a day trip to Minsmere in April 1959 and I still remember the thrill of watching my first marsh harrier quartering the reeds, against a backdrop of marshes and woodland. Since that first day, I have never failed to be thrilled by the sight of the extensive area of reeds and wetlands that meets the eye as one approaches Minsmere from the top of Dunwich Heath. So it was on our most recent trip, on a gloriously sunny morning, as we dropped down to walk along Minsmere beach.

The absence of saltings and the narrow beach give this part of the East Anglian coast a unique character, totally different from that with which we are so familiar in North Norfolk. Despite being November, the warm sun had encouraged a few red admirals and common darter dragonflies to take to the wing, although I doubt if they would have survived the severe wintry weather that was to occur only a couple of days later.

The large area of open water with scattered islands, that now seems to dominate the reserve at Minsmere, supported large numbers of wildfowl, principally teal and wigeon, with new arrivals appearing every so often from the east. Winter plumaged black-tailed godwits waded in the shallow water and well camouflaged snipe fed amongst the tussocks of sedge around the fringes of the pool.

In the far distance, the snow white dome of Sizewell B power station shone in the morning sun, and as Fran had never been there, we decided to drive down to take a closer look. The buildings of the two power stations are indeed most impressive at close quarters, not least because of their enormous size. Within the last year, the perimeter fence around the site on the seaward side has been moved back by about 50 yards. This has meant that the mature, if somewhat stunted, sycamores and an area of bushes and scrub can now be closely approached and checked for migrants. Dusky, Raddes and yellow-browed warblers have all been found there this autumn. Where the seawater used for cooling the plant is pumped back offshore, the temperature of the surrounding water is about three degrees higher and this attracts large numbers of gulls, which included a first-winter little gull on the day we were there.

Rain failed to spoil a fine walk in Suffolk

November 2001

As forecast, the spell of fine weather had broken by the time we awoke on the second day of our trip to Suffolk. Undeterred, Fran and I decided to visit English Nature's National Nature Reserve at Walberswick, as planned (Plate 8).

As we set off along the Suffolk Coast and Heaths Path, light rain was falling, which made the muddy track through the reeds at Walberswick, ever more slippery. With one eye on the path ahead and one scanning the sky, we had soon reached the derelict mill in the middle of the extensive reed-bed that stretched almost as far as the eye could see. To me there's something very special about being in the middle of a big reed-bed, surrounded on all sides by the closely packed stems of the *Phragmites*, their feathery flower heads gently swaying in the breeze. It's so easy to understand why the pioneering nature photographer, Emma Turner, wanted to spend so much time at Hickling in the early years of the last century.

Apart from occasional teal that sprung out of the network of dykes, few birds were seen and not even the squealing of a water rail broke the silence. Although a pomarine skua that crossed high over the reeds from the direction of the beach was an unexpected sighting. It was possibly the same bird that we had seen offshore at Sizewell, the previous day.

By the time we reached the beach, the rain had ceased and even the grey skies began to break to reveal scattered patches of blue. Our decision to come out, despite the weather, had been vindicated. Turning north, we walked along the low shingle ridge keeping a watchful eye on the string of small pools behind the beach. As well as the occasional redshank and dunlin, we found three fine, winter-plumaged spotted redshanks, swimming phalarope-like in one of the deeper pools, their long fine bills delicately picking morsels off the surface of the water. For one glorious moment, I thought I had found a party of Wilson's phalaropes, very rare vagrants from North America!

Two little egrets resting by one of the ditches was a pleasant surprise, although now they do seem to be a regular feature of many parts of the East Anglian coast. A woodcock that exploded from almost under our feet was clearly a recently arrived migrant, as were a few redwings and fieldfares that flew off inland.

The circular walk that had taken a couple of hours is one that we look forward to repeating in the summer.

In the bleak midwinter

Some birds do the strangest things

November 2001

During the summer Bev Cosse of the Seal and Bird Rescue Trust at Ridlington rang to tell me about the strange behaviour of a blackbird in her garden, the like of which I have never heard before.

A family of great spotted woodpeckers were regular visitors to a peanut holder hanging from an old hand pump in her garden, but their presence was clearly resented by a female blackbird nesting nearby. Whenever the woodpeckers arrived, the blackbird would fly to a nearby rose bed, pick off some petals of an orange-red rose, fly to where the woodpecker was feeding, sit on the water pump above the peanuts and proceed to shower the woodpecker with the petals! Apparently the same coloured rose was always chosen and the action had little effect on the feeding woodpeckers! I would be delighted to hear from any reader who has seen anything similar.

Another friend, John Butcher from Hellesdon, also rang with another amusing story about a neighbour who arrived home to find her Burmese cat showing considerable interest in the toaster in her kitchen. Closer inspection revealed a young house sparrow trapped inside. It appears that the cat had brought it in through the cat flap and, on escaping from the cat, the sparrow had sought refuge inside the toaster! Try as they might, they were unable to get the sparrow out and eventually the toaster had to be broken open to release it, much to the relief of the parent birds that were still waiting outside for their youngster.

Finally, last week I received a letter from John Eastbury of Cromer about a surprise visitor he found in his garage. Spread across the top of some cardboard boxes were the wings of a fairly large bird, which on closer inspection he discovered belonged to a sparrowhawk. The head of the bird was stuck through the base of the handles of a long-handled pair of lawn edging shears! The bird was very much alive and John was understandably very wary of its ferocious-looking bill. However, by simply opening the handles of the shears, the sparrowhawk was freed and gratefully flew away. It had clearly flown into the garage after a small bird - a case of the biter bit.

It's worth pointing out that it's actually the razor-sharp claws of birds of prey, which one should avoid. They are capable of striking with their feet at great speed, as I have discovered to my cost when handling kestrels and sparrowhawks for ringing!

Haven for wildlife shrouded in mist

December 1999

When I first arrived there last month, the eerie silence of Breydon Water, shrouded in mist, was broken only by the haunting cries of lapwings standing on the water's edge. As I walked along the footpath on the northern side, a rock pipit flitted from one of the dykes amongst the tangle of salt-marsh plants, giving its single, rather strident call. Fortunately my visit had coincided with a rising tide and as the water covered the mud, the available feeding area for waders was reduced, pushing them up towards me.

The estuary at Breydon is over four miles long and nearly a mile and a half wide, and the extensive mudflats exposed at low tide are the only areas of intertidal mud on the east coast of Norfolk. It's importance as a wildlife refuge has long been recognised and it is now designated as a Site of Special Scientific Interest by English Nature.

As I slowly continued on, a heron suddenly arose from a ditch uttering its startled call, while another stood sentinel-like on the edge of the tide waiting for any unsuspecting eel or fish. Each of the posts marking the channels, provided a convenient perch for a cormorant, many sitting with their wings held open.

Thousands of waders and ducks were visible on the remaining areas of exposed mud. As the tide rose noisy parties of dunlin began to retreat to the higher ground of the "lumps", where about 40 avocets were already resting and preening. Spangled grey plovers continued to feed sedately, occasionally uttering their plaintive calls, while there was an almost constant background sound of piping redshanks. A few knot and ringed plovers were scattered amongst the feeding waders, which were joined by two racing pigeons looking totally out of place.

As the birds were pushed even closer by the rising tide, I realised that the largest group of waders, made up of about 3000 birds were golden plover, a species that I normally associate with arable fields rather than muddy estuaries. It was interesting to see how the birds tended to remain in single species' flocks, rather than mixing. None more so than the groups of black-tailed godwits which were flying into the roosting area, and were instantly attracted by the calls of those already present.

At last a weak sun began to filter through the grey, overcast and mist-enshrouded Breydon, removing, as it did, some of the mystique of this haven for wildlife.

Heron struggled to swallow its meal

November 1999

On a recent visit to Breydon Water, I was amused to watch a heron attempting to swallow a dab that it had just caught. Eventually it was successful, but not until after much juggling and parading around. The first problem was how to manoeuvre the dab into a head-first position in its bill. This was achieved by occasionally shaking it and dunking it in the water, presumably to make it more slipperey, rather than to benefit the fish!

At last it was in the right position and the dab was ready to be swallowed. During this phase the heron stood motionless for several minutes, as if the effort had been particularly exhausting, before pointing its bill skywards, in the manner of a bittern, and allowing the dab to slowly pass down. The passage of the fish inside the heron's long neck was clearly visible and hardly had it finished before it was once more carefully stalking through the shallow water looking for its next meal!

I would have enjoyed the spectacle far less had it occurred in my garden, where a local heron, during the autumn, cleared my pond of goldfish. Although we never actually saw it catch a fish, on several occasions we saw it land near the pond and stealthily walk towards it. In an attempt to prevent it, I placed some garden twine around the pond set about 18in off the ground. Theoretically this is meant to stop a heron being able to walk to the edge of the water. However, on one occasion it was seen to walk underneath the twine with its head and neck held parallel to the ground. This prompted my wife to ask if I had ever before seen a heron duck!

In September, Judy Hawkins, an EDP reader from Bunwell, writing in a letter to the editor, reported a heron swimming on her pond, which is up to five feet deep in places. Although this observation was questioned by another correspondent, I'm sure Mrs Hawkins will be pleased to hear that her eyes weren't deceiving her. Herons are indeed quite accomplished, if infrequent, swimmers. One has even been observed catching a water vole by swimming after it.

In earlier times, herons would patrol the River Yare following the coasters and readily plunge head first into the river to seize any fish damaged by propellers. At such times only the heron's wings, which were held high, remained in view.

So many delights at Blakeney Harbour

December 2000

I always enjoy visiting harbours. Aside from the hustle and bustle of the quayside activity, there are inevitably gulls to be watched, with the chance of an occasional stranger amongst their midst. However, the water known as Blakeney Harbour, is totally different. A tidal area situated between Blakeney Point and Stiffkey Freshes, it is best approached from Morston, and it was from here, on a crystal clear morning earlier this month, that Fran and I set off from the National Trust car park. The tide was just on the turn and the seal boats were about to leave their quayside moorings. Rock pipits busily flitted along the edges of the creeks, occasionally flying up to land on a moored dingy, before disappearing into the hull to look for any tasty morsels. Interestingly, these small boats are also used by some of the pipits as roosting sites at night.

This part of Norfolk has an attraction all of its own. Salt marshes stretch westwards, as far as the eye can see, while inland the church towers of the coastal villages break the skyline at regular intervals; and then, of course, there is the expansive Norfolk sky.

A small group of restless twite, flitted nervously from the salt marsh, where they had been feeding on the seed-heads of sea aster, to drink at the edge of a freshwater pool. Like the rock pipits, these twite are winter visitors to Norfolk but from their moorland breeding homes in the north of England and Scotland. In appearance very similar to linnets, they differ in having a yellow bill and a distinctly nasal flight call.

We crossed rickety old wooden bridges over tortuous creeks, through which hurried the receding tide, and soon found ourselves slithering and sliding along the glistening mud towards the water's edge. Here hundreds, probably thousands, of waders and waterfowl were resting at their high-tide roosts. As the tide fell, they began to leave the higher ground in small groups and spill out onto the freshly exposed mud.

Tidal mud such as this produces more protein than the equivalent area of arable land - nature's own foodstore, which is so important to the winter survival of the 1.5 million waders that overwinter in Britain. A total that is about half of the entire European wader population! Diving in the deeper water of the harbour were small groups of red-breasted mergansers and goldeneyes, while a single scaup and slavonian grebe added further variety. But the highlight of this very pleasant walk was the sight of a male peregrine stooping playfully at the massed flocks of wheeling waders.

Mesmerised by large flocks of brent geese

February 2001

For me, the one bird that epitomises winter in North Norfolk is the brent goose. I never fail to be mesmerised by the large grazing flocks on the coastal marshes at Salthouse and Cley. Each flock tends to move as a single unit, usually with all the geese walking in one direction. This always reminds me of the dance-like display of flamingos, in which the birds change direction in unison. But within the group, there are also constant interactions. Often these are minor altercations between pairs, for brent geese maintain their pair bonds throughout the winter, and first-winter birds also remain within their own family groups.

I was recently watching a flock of about 800 at Cley, close enough for me to hear the characteristic incessant background noise of cackling and gentle squabbling. Young birds, easily recognised by the whitish tips to the upperwing coverts, resulting in narrow, pale bars across the upperparts, were surprisingly scarce. Only nine were present in this large flock, representing just over one per cent of the total. By estimating the percentage of these first-winter birds each year, it's possible to compare the annual breeding success of a species that's nesting as far away as Siberia. For that's where these dark-bellied brent geese, which overwinter in Norfolk, breed.

Last summer was clearly a poor breeding year for the brents, for in some winters the proportion of young birds can reach as high as 30 per cent. These successful breeding seasons frequently follow a three-year cycle and coincide with those years when high numbers of lemmings are present on the breeding grounds. The lemmings provide a good source of food for the Arctic foxes, whereas when lemmings are in short supply, the foxes feed their cubs on the goslings.

Brent geese have not always been so numerous in North Norfolk. During the nineteenth century, no more than 300 could normally be found at Blakeney, feeding on the salt-marsh plant, eel-grass *Zostera marina*. During the 1930s, the world population of dark-bellied brent geese crashed dramatically, believed to be related to a failure of the eel-grass. However, it is now thought that the decline was due to the collection of eggs and flightless, moulting adult geese to feed the inmates of Stalin's gulag camps! Whatever the cause, the brent goose population is now extremely healthy as demonstrated by the many thousands which overwinter in North Norfolk.

Hedgerow larder of fruit and nuts

December 2000

While driving along a narrow country lane last week, I was delighted to see a party of redwings and fieldfares gorging themselves on the ripe fruits of a hedgerow. This brought home to me the importance of the correct management of one of our declining, and yet so important, types of habitat. A subject recently touched on by fellow columnist, Rex Hancy.

Every reader will be aware of the dramatic loss of hedgerows since the second world war. What is, perhaps, less appreciated is the fact that hedges are not a "natural" part of our landscape. Several thousand years ago, as woods were felled and cleared to create fields for crops, strips of woodland were left to mark the field boundaries and later to keep in grazing livestock. These now form our oldest hedgerows and many delineate the present parish boundaries.

Although new hedges have been planted for at least 2000 years, a large proportion of our long-established hedgerows date from the time of the first Enclosure Act of 1603 and onwards. There is a useful rule of thumb that can be used in trying to roughly estimate the age of an old hedge - each species of established shrub or tree, counted on one side of a 30-yard length of hedge, represents about one hundred years.

So returning to my original point, how best can a hedgerow be managed to optimise its value to wildlife?

As with all countryside issues, a compromise has to be reached that is satisfactory to environmental, farming, and in this case, highway needs. For wildlife, thick hedges with wide bases, containing a good variety of woody species along with some standard trees, such as oaks, are the best. These have plenty of cover for nesting, feeding and roosting birds, the taller trees provide song posts, while holes in the older trees can be used by bats, as well as birds. The thick tangle at the base will be a haven for insects, while if seeds are allowed to set wild flowers will grow in profusion on either side of the hedge.

Many hedges do need to be trimmed annually and nowadays this is usually carried out with a flail trimmer, but it is the timing of this work that is so important. Hedges should never be cut between March and August, (the nesting season for birds) and the work is best left until the end of winter, after the wildlife larder of fruits and nuts has been emptied.

Thrushes are part of a global family

March 2001
Although we may think of thrushes as being typically British birds, they are members of one of the most widely distributed families in the world. In fact, there are over 60 species in the genus *Turdus*, which are regarded by most people as typical thrushes, and representatives can be found on every continent.

Both fieldfares and redwings are winter visitors to Britain but it is generally not until February or March that really large flocks occur in East Anglia. In recent years, fieldfares have tended to be more numerous than redwings, with flocks containing several hundred birds being reported from many parts of the region. About the size of mistle thrushes, and again like them, in having a very upright stance, fieldfares are readily recognised by their pale grey head and rump that is particularly noticeable in flight. Almost invariably they also give their characteristic "tchack, tchack" call as they take to the wing.

The largest flocks are normally found on grazing meadows, where they feed on earthworms, slugs and insects. Unlike redwings, they also take advantage of any fallen fruit, especially apples, but are normally only seen in gardens during periods of severe weather. In the last few weeks, I have come across many such flocks, throughout North Norfolk, usually with a handful of redwings accompanying them.

At one time, the most likely identity of a "strange" bird reported in a non-bird-watcher's garden, would have been a redwing - "It's just like a thrush, but has red on the side and a white eye-stripe." Such reports occur less frequently now, possibly because the milder winters have meant that fewer redwings are visiting gardens. In common with fieldfares, redwings also have a very distinct flight call, a thin "tseep", which is also used at night to enable individual birds within a migrating flock to remain in contact with each other.

Both species breed widely in central and northern Europe, with many of our winter visitors in East Anglia coming from Scandinavia. This is one reason for the large numbers, often found in late winter and early spring, only a few miles inland from the Norfolk coast - the birds are gathering prior to their spring return across the North Sea.

Although occasional redwings and fieldfares will linger well into late spring, and have even been found in mid-summer, neither species has ever been proved to breed in Norfolk. Fieldfares nest in close proximity to each other, and observers entering such a breeding colony, do so at their own risk. Apparently the birds dive-bomb intruders, dropping excrement with incredible accuracy!

So much to see at Holkham Reserve

December 1999

The Holkham National Nature Reserve is particularly worth a visit or two during the winter months and I had a most enjoyable trip there in early December. Despite a surprisingly cold, south-westerly wind and rather overcast skies, I was able to see a very good selection of those species which overwinter regularly in the county, as well as a real rarity.

I never tire of watching the flocks of wild geese which feed, often only a stone's throw away, in the field to the east of Lady Ann's Drive. On this particular morning several hundred pink-footed geese were grazing, apparently unconcerned by the nearby cars. The birds were clearly sticking together in family parties, the adults looking especially smart, their blue-grey upperparts barred paler, while the larger ganders were clearly dominant. Although vast numbers of this species, which breeds in Iceland, formerly wintered in the Holkham area, it is only since the mid-1980s that once again it has become abundant here. There were constant comings and goings amongst the flock, with skeins of both white-fronted and brent geese flying down to join the ever active pink-feet. At any one time, some individuals would always be looking around with head raised, to warn the others if danger threatened.

Seeking the shelter of the seaward side of the pines, I walked along the tideline, as ever marvelling at the fact that despite visiting Holkham on many occasions, I have yet to see the tide in. Clearly it does rise, as evidenced by the seaweed and other debris only a few yards from the dunes! I was delighted to find feeding amongst the salt-marsh plants a mixed flock of shore larks (or should I call them horned larks, as we are now encouraged to do!) and twite. Shore larks are always a pleasure to watch with their striking black and yellow face markings, which in the male's breeding plumage are enhanced by a pair of devil-like horns, from which the species gets its alternative name.

While watching these, a twinkling party of snow buntings flew past, which like the shore larks are mountain-top breeders and are only found along the coast in winter. But the most exciting bird of the day, a desert wheatear, was yet to be located. Present since late November, it favoured an area of beach near the western end of Holkham pines. It was well worth the long walk to see this very tame, sandy-coloured wheatear, which had only been recorded in Norfolk on nine previous occasions.

Turnstone - a bird that lives up to its name

February 2000

While walking along the promenade at Sheringham this month I was able to appreciate an additional benefit provided by the large rocks at the base of the concrete wall. Brought over from Scandinavia a couple of years ago, they were manoeuvred into position to strengthen the sea defences. Since then bladder wrack and other seaweeds have colonised the surface of the rocks, amongst which a variety of sea creatures now hide. This in turn, has created an additional habitat on which turnstones and purple sandpipers can feed. Two species of wader that are more characteristic of the rocky coasts of northern and western Britain.

Turnstones are regular winter visitors to the Sheringham beaches. About the size of blackbirds, they can be readily identified by their grey-brown upperparts and breast, contrasting with white below. Their legs and feet are orange and in flight they show a distinct black and white, so-called harlequin wing pattern. Their diet is surprisingly varied compared with many other waders and they are just as happy poking among seaweed looking for small crustacea and molluscs, as turning over the pebbles on the beach to search for hidden morsels. Their slightly upturned bill is admirably designed for flipping over small stones and it is, of course, from this behaviour that the species acquired its name.

Several years ago, taking advantage of the fact that turnstones will eat a wide variety of food items, I decided to try and catch some for ringing, on the Leas at Sheringham. I baited an area with bread and set up a small clap net, and sure enough this proved irresistible to about a dozen, which I duly caught. However, news spreads fast in a small town and it wasn't long before Isabel Bateman, who I believe was the secretary of the local branch of the RSPCA, had been summoned to investigate someone catching birds on the promenade! When she realised it was only me, she became as fascinated as all the other bystanders, at the chance to see the birds in the hand.

For several winters, some of the turnstones that I ringed that day came back each autumn to Sheringham for their "winter holidays". As a result of ringing large numbers of turnstones on The Wash, many of which were subsequently recovered, we know that they return each summer to breed in Greenland, and some even as far away as Ellesmere Island in Canada. This will also be the case with those we see each winter at Sheringham.

Braving the cold to enjoy a rare sight

December 1999

I don't chase after rare birds and so by definition I'm not a twitcher. But I was unable to resist making a trip to Aldeburgh in Suffolk in mid-December to see an ivory gull that had turned up a few days earlier. As this was the only species of gull to have been recorded in Britain that I had not seen before, I felt that my action was justified! Strangely enough, the last time that I had "twitched" a bird outside Norfolk was also a gull in Suffolk - the Franklin's gull from North America that overwintered in the Lowestoft area in 1977-78.

So, 20 years after last chasing a bird outside my home county, I found myself on a bitterly cold morning outside the White Lion Hotel at Aldeburgh. If I'd had more sense, I would have been inside warming the inner man!

The conditions, of course, were perfect for the ivory gull, which is a resident of the High Arctic, usually staying near the pack ice throughout the year. In fact, it ranges further north than any other species of bird. Here I was able to enjoy spectacular views of this attractive bird, at times down to about 20ft.

When on the ground it was remarkably pigeon-like, with a rounded body, short neck and short, black legs. Being a first-winter bird, its gleaming white plumage was flecked with a few fine black spots, as were the tips of the flight feathers and the tail, while blackish feathers around its face gave it an almost ruffian-like appearance (Plate 9).

Every couple of hours it fed greedily on codling that had been discarded around the fishermen's huts and boats, skilfully extracting the contents of the chest and abdominal cavities through a small hole below the gills. After gorging, it sat hunched up on the pebbles, fitfully dozing, while occasional drips could be seen collecting, and then falling, from the tip of its bill. In common with other seabirds, ivory gulls possess well-developed nasal glands that excrete a strong saline solution, thus maintaining normal salt levels in the blood and body tissues. It was this solution that could be seen dripping from the end of its bill.

Although the species is now recorded almost annually in Britain, the vast majority are seen in the Northern Isles and it is very unlikely that I will ever have the chance of seeing one in East Anglia again. I wonder what the New Year will bring?

Season's greetings from robin redbreast

December 1999

I wonder how many readers have wondered why the robin features on so many of our Christmas cards? Writing this regular column has encouraged me to research just this sort of question.

The robin has always been held in great respect throughout the country, and there are many traditional versions of the problems associated with harming or killing one. These have included a persistent trembling of the hands, sickness and even the loss of a limb. The Anglo-Saxon name for a robin was "rudduc", a reference to the colour of its breast. By the Middle Ages it was widely known as "redbreast", the prefix Robin simply being a nickname, an abbreviation of Robert. Indeed it was only during the twentieth century that the name "robin" was accepted as the official name for our most-loved bird.

As an indication of its popularity, it was mentioned by William Wordsworth in no less than 14 of his poems, perhaps the most famous lines being:

Art thou the bird whom man loves best,
The pious bird with the scarlet breast,
Our little English Robin?

One aspect of a robin's behaviour, however, may not endear it to many people, although it is only following a human trait, and that is its zealous defence of its territory. Although most disputes are confined to posturing and chasing each other, robins do occasionally get involved in physical contests, where the rivals grapple each other with their feet entwined and peck vigorously at each others heads. These engagements have even been known to end in the death of one of the birds.

In autumn, young robins, unlike many other species, begin to stake out territories that are defended against other robins, and these may well include visitors from other parts of Europe. Although "our" robins are generally non-migratory, those breeding in Scandinavia and central Europe do move south in the autumn, and some of these pass through Norfolk. Edna Higson of Overstrand wrote to me about just such a situation in October, when her garden was alive with robins being harried by the local birds.

But returning to my original question about the robin at Christmas, one of the reasons is that early postmen wore bright red waistcoats, and were widely known as "robins". As a result, the robin featured on some of the earliest Christmas cards, and was often shown with a letter in its bill, actually delivering the mail!

Natural antifreeze protects butterflies

December 1999

To me, summer really has arrived when I see my first red admiral and painted lady butterflies, generally in late May or early June. Both of these closely related species arrive in Britain after journeys of up to 600 miles from the warmer climes of the Mediterranean, with the painted lady having travelled from as far away as North Africa. But when autumn comes, these butterflies are unable to survive the cold winters of northern Europe, and either have to migrate south or else perish, as most of them do.

However, most of the other species seen in Norfolk are able to overwinter and they do this in a variety of ways. A few, such as the Essex skipper and purple hair-streak, overwinter in the egg stage. The amount of daylight and the ambient temperature controlling whether the egg develops and hatches within a few days, or else remains dormant until the following spring. The commonest method of surviving the winter is as a caterpillar, as do most of the browns, fritillaries, blues (Plate 9) and small copper. Some, for example the small skippers, eat only their egg case before going into hibernation as very tiny caterpillars. This ability to withstand low winter temperatures is due to the presence within their blood of natural antifreeze, which will protect them down to temperatures as low as -14C.

Other species, such as the large white, overwinters as a chrysalis. The final caterpillar stage is able to accurately measure the number of daylight hours per day. If there are more than 15 hours, then the caterpillar will turn into a chrysalis which will emerge as a butterfly a couple of weeks later. However, if there are less than 15 hours of daylight, the butterfly will not emerge from the chrysalis until the following spring, which may be as long as nine months away.

Most people will have come across hibernating butterflies during the winter months, most often small tortoiseshells or peacocks. As autumn progresses both of these species will enter buildings to seek out a quiet, cool corner in which to hibernate. During this time their metabolism slows right down and they survive on their body fat reserves. Like the overwintering caterpillars, their blood contains the sugar, sorbitol, which acts as an antifreeze. Far fewer people, though, will have found a brimstone or comma butterfly hibernating. They do not enter buildings, but rather rely on camouflage to conceal themselves amongst leaves, in order to avoid the attention of predators.

Surprised at seeing a quail in midwinter

February 2000

One of the great joys of birdwatching is its unpredictability - you never know what you're going to see next!

At the end of January, I was surveying the cliff-top fields between Sheringham and Weybourne for the Norfolk Bird Atlas. A loose flock of over 40 pied wagtails feeding in a field where the sugar beet had recently been lifted, came as a pleasant surprise, as did a pair of grey partridges, a species which it is not always easy to find in this area. Having already noted a covey of eight red-legged partridges and a few pheasants, I was pleased to have "completed" my list of game birds.

However, as I crossed an unusually weedy, stubble field, counting the skylarks that were taking advantage of this unploughed oasis, a small brown bird, with whirring wings took off from a few yards in front of me, and flew low across the field. I could scarcely believe my eyes - a quail! About half the size of a partridge and with distinct pale stripes on its back, there was no mistaking this rarity! I also heard for the first time ever, its rather quiet flight call of "cruck, cruck, cruck".

Apart from the fact that quail are normally only heard and not seen, they are also summer visitors to the British Isles and so finding one in the middle of winter was an added bonus. Although winter records in Norfolk during the nineteenth century appear to have been fairly frequent, there have only been four in recent years. But perhaps this is simply a reflection of the decline in numbers of quail generally.

Certainly, the spectacular "falls" of migratory quail that were noted around the Mediterranean in earlier years, appear to be a thing of the past. One of the most dramatic was recorded in the book of Numbers in the Old Testament: "And there went forth a wind from the Lord, and brought quails from the sea, and let them fall by the camp...". As a result of this unexpected source of food, Moses and the Children of Israel were able to survive during their flight from Egypt.

In fact, one of the earliest written references to bird migration also appears in the Bible, in the book of Jeremiah: "Yea, the stork in the heaven knoweth her appointed times; and the turtle and the crane and the swallow observe the time of their coming."

Readers are keen to keep me up to date

February 2001

Recently I wrote about the responses following my earlier article on Arthur Patterson. But it wasn't only that column which provided some interesting letters from readers. Just the mention of local Norfolk names for birds, or in the case of the dunnock, an apparent absence of local names, and a reaction is almost guaranteed!

Ron Fiske of Morningthorpe sent me a list of no less than 12 Norfolk names for the dunnock, and I hadn't been able to find a single one! Amongst them was "Hedge Betty", which is very close to "Hedgey bet" that Tony Cardy of Kenninghall remembered being used in South Norfolk in the 1940s. This is also the name that Maisie Martin of Downham Market sent me, only recently having come across the name dunnock, for the first time.

Several people have also contacted me about changes in the feeding habits of certain garden birds. As I mentioned last month, long-tailed tits are now regularly recorded feeding on peanuts, but Ian Billings wrote to tell me about some in his garden at Matishall feeding on the ground. Since Christmas, about 20 long-tailed tits have spent long periods in a hedge between his garden and an adjoining field. While on several occasions they have fed on bread crumbs and pastry placed on the patio. At least twice, ten were feeding together on a 15in-square patio slab. So intrigued was he by this, that the washing-up water went cold while he watched! Strangely enough, I also saw long-tailed tits foraging on the ground for the first time in January, as a party of them worked along a bank at the base of a hedge.

Paul Banham of Wells has also been fascinated by the evolving behaviour of birds at garden feeders. In a note, he commented that only a few years ago, tits and greenfinches were the only birds capable of feeding at nut dispensers, whereas in his garden the commonest now are house sparrows, which must be unusual nowadays, and starlings, while it was as recent as last December that he first recorded long-tailed tits on peanuts. The latest development is a blackbird which launches itself at a suspended fat-ball (it doesn't attempt to grab hold of it) and then goes down to collect what it has knocked off! Now that really is enterprising!

Finally, John Butcher of Norwich rang to say that he had a report of a goldcrest that was feeding from a nut dispenser, which could well be a "first"; unless of course any reader knows different!

A winter visit to Cockshoot Broad

February 2001

One morning in late January, David Gafford of Salhouse rang to say that he thought he'd seen a drake canvasback, a rare North American duck, on the River Bure near Cockshoot Broad. As it was a sunny and crisp winter's day, and we had nothing planned, Fran and I decided to visit that part of Broadland, in the hope of finding the duck and being able to confirm the sighting.

Up to then, the weather in January had been pretty miserable, and so we particularly enjoyed the drive from Sheringham under a blue sky with cotton wool clouds skudding across in the brisk southerly wind. Farmers were also clearly taking advantage of the better weather, with ploughing much in evidence, but our journey was brought to a sudden halt, when we spotted a large mass of birds wheeling over a stubble field. As suddenly as they had appeared, they dropped from view behind the roadside bank, and on stopping I discovered them resting on some recently ploughed land. As I had suspected they were golden plovers (Plate 10), their spangled upperparts highlighted in the bright sun. But what did surprise me, was the size of the flock, which I estimated to contain about 1200 birds - a good-sized flock of golden plovers by any standard!

It didn't take us long to reach Woodbastwick and we were soon walking along the boardwalk that runs by the side of the Bure and leads towards Cockshoot Broad. A few great crested grebes were on the river, quite unconcerned by our presence only a short distance away, while a water rail screamed from the nearby reeds. Following the excellent boardwalk we were soon walking through the alder carr that leads to the broad. This is the ideal habitat for the willow tit, a species that has become extremely scarce in Norfolk in recent years. Although we didn't find any, we did come across a pair of marsh tits, which are very similar in appearance.

Cockshoot Broad has been the target of a special conservation project that has enabled it to be returned to its former glory. This has been achieved by building a dam to isolate it from the polluted waters of the River Bure and by dredging tons of mud from the broad. Fran and I both agreed that it was certainly an area we would like to return to in the spring.

Unfortunately, we were not able to find the canvasback, although I was surprised to discover a fulvous whistling duck dozing on the river bank, not a European species, and clearly an escape from a nearby wildfowl collection.

Hoarders ensure they will not go hungry

December 1999

For several weeks in late autumn, up to three jays were making regular flights over my garden, transporting acorns from a nearby oak tree. Jays, in common with several other members of the crow family, are great food hoarders and these birds were collecting the acorns to store them up for use in the winter. The gullet of the jay is unusually large, thus enabling it to carry several acorns at once, in addition to the one that is often seen held in the bird's bill. The acorns are then individually buried in the ground at the selected site, from where they will be subsequently retrieved up to many weeks later. As some of the acorns will inevitably remain uneaten, the jay is thus an important propagator of oak trees.

The habit of food hoarding occurs in several bird families, notably the birds of prey (including owls), woodpeckers, tits, nuthatches and shrikes, as well as the crows. One has only to watch the frequent visits of a coal tit to a peanut or sunflower seed holder on a bird table, to realise that the bird could not possibly be eating all the seeds which it's rapidly taking away. Most will be stored in sites such as crevices in bark, holes in trees or even unopened rose buds, as was happening in my garden one autumn.

One of the best-known hoarders of food, in the bird world, must be the red-backed shrike (Plate 10). Surplus insects, such as beetles, and vertebrates, such as lizards, are impaled on the spikes of hawthorn bushes, for later use. This cache of food is known as the shrike's "larder" and this habit earned the shrike its alternative name of "butcher bird".

The nutcracker, a member of the crow family and a rare irruptive visitor to the British Isles from central and northern Europe, collects large numbers of hazelnuts during the autumn. These it stores in caches of up to 20 nuts on the ground, which it covers up with vegetation. Careful observation has demonstrated that the birds are able to locate these food stores very accurately and that their subsequent discovery is not simply a matter of chance. Saplings and other trees appear to be used as markers to guide the nutcrackers to their stores. Even several inches of snow on the ground does not prevent the food from being rapidly found. Perhaps more remarkable, these stores are used to feed nestlings the following spring, proving that the birds can remember their location after several months.

Fishermen share catch with turnstones

March 2001

On one of the few, warm and sunny days this winter, Fran and I decided to walk along a stretch of the ancient Peddars Way, that also forms part of the Norfolk Coast Path. Although we had driven along the coast road that runs parallel to this section, on many occasions, we had never before taken the footpath. Starting at the village of Burnham Deepdale, we followed the path westwards along the coast, before it cut inland at Brancaster.

The setting could not have been better, for despite being mid-February, the sky was blue, the sun shone brightly and scarcely a breeze pulled at the pennants on the boats riding in the creeks. On the far side of the salt marsh, almost a mile away, the island of Scolt Head was clearly visible. Despite its relative proximity, to most of us it remains a place of mystery and tales of rare birds seen by just a lucky few.

We had arrived at the top of the tide, and the creeks and main channels were full, with the water virtually motionless and hardly a ripple to be seen on the surface. The still air was broken only by the occasional bubbling call of a curlew, as it took off, responding to some potential threat, of which we were unaware. Despite their size, curlews are easily overlooked at a distance, their brown plumage providing good camouflage against the backdrop of the saltings. Large flocks of lapwings were taking the opportunity to roost on the comparative safety of the salt marsh, their iridescent green and purple upperparts glinting in the strong sun. Like many waders, lapwings roost at high tide, in order to make the most of the ideal feeding conditions at low water, whether by day or night.

At Brancaster Staithe, the mussel fishermen were sorting and washing their catch, with small groups of turnstones constantly running around near them, in the hope of picking up some tasty morsels, which include shore crabs and any broken mussels. This association between turnstones and shell-fishing has become well established in North Norfolk over many centuries, whether it's oysters, cockles, whelks or, as today, mussels that are being gathered. By the end of March these same birds will be on their long journey north to their breeding grounds in the high Canadian Arctic and Greenland.

Beyond Brancaster Staithe, the walking became easier, along a raised boardwalk made out of old railway sleepers. This was bordered on the seaward side by reed-beds, which in only a few weeks time would once again be alive with the songs of reed and sedge warblers.

Every leg tells a story in the bird world

November 2001
In much the same way that the structure of a bird's bill tells us about its feeding habits, so the legs and feet provide information about a bird's lifestyle. Anatomically, the part of a bird's lower limb that we call its "leg" is actually formed out of bones from the upper foot, and is really equivalent to parts of our ankle. Whereas the comparable bones to our lower and upper legs are both hidden by feathers within the bird's flanks.

In general, birds that possess short legs tend to hop, while those with long legs walk or run. Those that are capable of running the fastest, such as the ostrich and cassowary, have the longest legs of all, which is a vital adaptation to being flightless, as speed across the ground is of major importance. Certain wading birds, stilts and flamingos for example, are characterised by unusually long legs that enable them to feed in deeper water without getting their plumage wet. The shortest legs are found in those birds that rarely walk, the swifts and kingfishers.

Similarly, the structure of the feet is adapted to the habitat in which each bird lives. Most land species have what would be considered to be typical bird's feet: long, widely separated toes, three pointing forwards and one back. This configuration, however, is different in the woodpeckers, in which there are two toes pointing in each direction. This adaptation enables the woodpeckers to more easily clamber up the trunks and along the boughs. Such an arrangement is known as zygodactyl, from the Greek meaning "yoke toed".

Many water birds, on the other hand, have webbed feet, the legs and feet being used as paddles when swimming (Plate 11). To further enhance propulsion, the legs in certain families, like the divers, are set further back on the body. In fact, they are set so far back that walking is virtually impossible. On land, a bird such as the red-throated diver, has to wriggle along on its belly. Between these two extremes, grebes are provided with lobed toes, which are twisted sideways as the legs move forwards while swimming, in much the same way that an oarsman feathers his blades.

But the strangest structural features found in the feet of certain birds are the comb-like pectinate claws. These are present in some members of the heron family, where they are probably used in preening, but their function in nightjars and pratincoles is less easily explained.

Long-tailed tits' winter survival strategy

January 2001

I'm sure that every reader enjoys seeing long-tailed tits, as much as I do. My earliest bird records, made while I was at school in Essex, show that I first saw one in February 1957. Without doubt, this would have involved one of those winter parties, which are often heard well before they are seen. The distinct, trilling call given by the individuals within the flock, is used to remain in contact with each other, and is a sound that never fails to please. These winter parties, which usually consist of six to eight individuals, but can be considerably larger, are almost certainly one or more family groups that have remained together since the breeding season. The largest flock in Norfolk in recent years was one of 65 at Sennowe Park in November 1997.

Detailed studies have shown that in winter such parties of long-tailed tits hold group territories, each covering an area of about 20 hectares. Within this area, the flock will move a distance of about seven kilometres during the course of a winter's day. No wonder then that they always seem to be on the move!

Their diminutive body size (like a small fluffy ball) and disproportionately long tail, make them easy to recognise, as does the delicate pink patch on their back. Their small size, however, creates problems of survival during cold weather. For this reason, they need to spend 90 per cent of their day actively searching for food. As they are largely insectivorous, this can create problems during the winter.

As in other species of birds, long-tailed tits learn by example, and in recent years more and more are being seen feeding from suspended fat-balls and peanut holders in gardens. This change in behaviour, along with the recent run of mild winters, is thought to be behind the increasing numbers of long-tailed tits in Britain at the present time. This is just part of a longer-term trend that has been demonstrated by the British Trust for Ornithology, during the last 15 years.

However, it's during the course of very cold winter nights that long-tailed tits are most likely to suffer. Unlike other members of the tit family, they don't roost in holes, but huddle up together in clumps on a small branch, often inside a thick evergreen shrub. In my garden, I most often see them in late afternoon, feeding on the peanuts. Then they silently fly off as a group, in a straight line to some secret hideaway, where they know they'll be safe until morning.

Titchwell trip on one of those lucky days

March 2000

Despite the bright morning sun, the westerly breeze produced quite a nip in the air, when I visited the RSPB's Titchwell Reserve in late February. Although my last visit in January had been unusually disappointing, it was to be different on this occasion.

I was greeted with the bubbling call of a curlew, while a lone skylark was singing his heart out, high in the sky above me. As I started along the path on the bund, that separates the saltwater marsh from the fresh marshes, three little egrets flapped slowly out of one of the saltwater dykes only to disappear again a few hundred yards away. I wonder how long it will be before these recent British colonists will be added to the county's list of breeding birds?

It wasn't long before I had also managed to locate the resident black-winged stilt, vying with a nearby avocet for the title of most elegant black and white wader. Black-winged stilts are normally very rare visitors to Britain, but this particular individual first arrived at nearby Snettisham Pits in August 1993, moving to Titchwell after a few days, where it has remained ever since! Such an extended stay is unique in British ornithological history, but there is no real evidence that it is anything other than a genuinely wild bird.

As it was a morning tide, I decided to walk directly to the beach and it wasn't long before I had arrived at the observation platform, joining a group of similarly minded seawatchers. Amongst them was my old friend Ray Kimber, former golf professional at Brancaster. A life-long birdwatcher, Ray now devotes much of his time to voluntary work at the Titchwell Reserve. During the two hours that he had been seawatching he had recorded over 600 little gulls moving west, in groups of up to about 40, with many flying only a hundred yards or so offshore. As I stood with him, another noisy party flew along, consisting of a mixture of adult and first-winter birds. The black underwing of the adults contrasted beautifully with the dove grey sky, while some were also beginning to show the black hood of their summer plumage.

Close inshore, two pairs of long-tailed ducks and two slavonian grebes joined the loose flock of goldeneyes and eiders, frequently diving in the surf. As I remarked to him, birding is rather like golf. When luck is with you, everything falls into place, even those long putts drop into the hole!

Flying visitors from the northern forests

April 2001
Siskins are birds that have become increasingly familiar to garden birdwatchers in recent years. Their confiding nature and attraction to peanuts have made them firm favourites in many gardens. Considerably smaller than the stocky greenfinch, the male siskin is readily identified by its bright yellow face, breast, rump and wing-bars, contrasting with the black crown and white belly. The female is a duller, more streaky version of the male.

Prior to the 1960s, siskins were largely confined to the coniferous forests of northern and central Europe, and in the British Isles to Scotland and Ireland. But in winter 1963, a few were noted for the first time feeding on peanuts in gardens in Surrey. During the course of the next few years, this habit became more widespread and by 1971 siskins had been recorded on peanuts in Norfolk gardens.

As in many other species, for example long-tailed tits, new food sources and methods of feeding are learnt by example and it was not long before many Norfolk gardens were hosting these attractive birds. In fact, Michael Seago, writing in this column in 1994, made an appeal for readers to report sightings of siskins feeding in their gardens and at their bird tables; a request which brought in no fewer than 156 positive responses! This was no doubt related to the exceptional influx into Norfolk during autumn 1993.

Because of the large numbers present, a county-wide ringing study was conducted in Norfolk between January and April 1994. During this four-month period, over 3000 siskins were ringed in Norfolk gardens (including 580 in my own garden in Sheringham) and many interesting facts emerged. The two most important garden features which appeared to be necessary to attract large numbers were firstly mature trees that provided perches for loafing, preening and singing, which in turn proved an attraction to overflying birds, and secondly a small pond at which the siskins could drink. Recoveries of the ringed birds from 1994 indicated that they had originated from the Continent, as well as Northumberland and Scotland.

The more observant readers will have noticed that siskins rarely appear in Norfolk gardens until the New Year, and often not until well into February. During the first half of winter, they feed on the seeds of alders and birches, and it is only when these natural food supplies have been exhausted that they turn their attention to the alternative food sources provided in our gardens. This winter, the first appeared in my garden in early March, with up to 16 present by the end of the month.

Take a fresh look at the magpie

October 1999

Probably the most hated bird in Norfolk is the magpie, and readers may be surprised to hear that I actually enjoy seeing them in my garden! Unfortunately they have received a very bad press over recent years and have been blamed for the decline in many of our common garden songbirds. To my eyes, they are particularly handsome birds, as are most species which are black and white, especially when the sun catches their glossy green-black plumage. While their long tails add elegance to their characteristic flight, during which rapid bursts of wing flapping are interspersed with short glides.

During the nineteenth century, magpies were extremely scarce in Norfolk and it was only as a result of the reduced activities of gamekeepers that they came back from the brink of extinction as a breeding species in the county. Nowadays, they are found in a great variety of habitats, although where persecution is low, they prefer to breed near towns, villages and farms. For the size of the bird, magpie nests are unusually bulky (particularly those built by older, more experienced pairs) and the majority are roofed with an impenetrable dome, to protect the contents from crows.

The reproductive behaviour of magpies has been studied for many years in the Midlands by a team of students from Sheffield University led by Professor Tim Birkhead. They have found that monogamy in magpies, is not as common as had traditionally been thought. Around the period of egg-laying the male magpie tries never to let the female out of his sight, following her every move. This is to prevent her from being tempted by the sexual advances of the males in the adjacent territories.

Despite suggestions to the contrary, magpies have never been proved to have had a detrimental effect on the overall breeding success of other bird species. Indeed, research has found that their diet consists mainly of invertebrates in the summer and plant material in the winter, with only a minority of individuals taking any birds or eggs. Although I suspect that many readers will be able to provide first-hand accounts of such behaviour!

I would be particularly interested to hear from anyone who has evidence of magpies approaching or breaking open house martin nests to steal the young. On one house in West Sussex, six such nests were all attacked in this way and English Nature is interested to know if a similar problem exists elsewhere.

Overseas' travels

Trinidad is a birdwatchers' paradise

September 1999

I've recently returned from a birdwatching trip to Trinidad and Tobago, the two most southerly islands in the Caribbean chain. Although politically a single unit, the two islands are very different, as far as the birds are concerned. Trinidad lies only seven miles off the coast of Venezuela and geologically is part of South America. Half of the island is forested, and in the north, where we stayed, there is a range of low mountains, peaking at just over 3000ft. For a comparatively small island (under 2000 square miles) the diversity of wildlife is amazing.

Perhaps the most famous birds of Trinidad are the scarlet ibises. A must for any visitor to the island has to be a boat trip on the mangrove swamp at Caroni. While slowly passing along the narrow channels, through the otherwise impenetrable red mangroves, the keen-eyed boatman pointed out a whole range of wildlife. Cayman, small members of the alligator family, slid silently beneath the surface as the boat approached; while Cook's tree boas, one of the many species of snake in Trinidad (most of which are non-poisonous), garlanded themselves around the branches of the mangroves.

As we approached the more open areas of water in the middle of the swamp, the first few flights of scarlet ibis began to appear. These dazzlingly red birds, related to the herons, flew low over us in line astern, in parties of up to 30. As the sun began to set and the sky turned orange, more and more arrived to roost in the safety of the extensive and inaccessible mangroves. Perhaps surprisingly, many of these birds make the daily return journey from feeding grounds in Venezuela.

Nestling amongst the rain forest of the Northern Range of Trinidad is the world-famous Asa Wright Nature Centre, an absolute paradise for birdwatchers and indeed naturalists of any persuasion. Here we stayed in the comfortably furnished lodge, originally built as the estate-house.

Each day began at 6am with coffee on the veranda while watching the first arrivals at the feeding stations below. Chestnut woodpeckers and various species of tanager voraciously attacked the bananas, pineapple slices and other fruit put out daily for the birds. Hummingbirds and honeycreepers drank from the feeders filled with sugared water, while channel-billed toucans with their outrageously large bills, delicately picked fruit from the trees of the nearby rain forest.

Despite visiting Trinidad during the wet season, we were very fortunate with the weather; but when it rained - boy did it rain!

The forest giants of British Columbia

October 1999

My wife and I have recently returned from a memorable holiday in Canada, during which we travelled the breadth of this vast country on the Transcanadian train. After flying into Vancouver, we spent a week in the western province of British Columbia. Much of the land is still covered in extensive stands of mature conifers and many of the trees reach truly gigantic proportions, with some standing over 300ft high! The remains of one that we saw on Vancouver Island had a diameter of 11ft 6in and from the annual growth rings had been calculated to have been 1340 years old!

The characteristic bird of these western forests was the chestnut-backed chickadee - a coal tit-like bird with warm chestnut upperparts and flanks. Being autumn, however, the woodlands were generally quiet and surprisingly few birds were encountered. I was particularly keen to see Steller's jay (Plate 11), which replaces the blue jay in the west. On Vancouver Island we were treated to a family party of four feeding on picnic leftovers. About the size of our jays, they were a most attractive deep blue colour, their heads adorned with a large crest.

But it was the seabirds that I was especially looking forward to seeing. Although the cliff-nesting birds had already left their colonies, some were still feeding in the inshore waters. Some were familiar, such as the guillemot, others new to me, for example the marbled murrelet and rhinoceros auklet (surely one of the most bizarre bird names?). Identifying the many species of gulls was a real challenge. At Clover Point, on the southern tip of Vancouver Island, no less than eight species were present one morning. These included the locally-breeding glaucous-winged gulls, Californian gulls that breed hundreds of miles inland but winter along the coast, and Heermann's gulls, the immatures of which are uniformly dark brown, thus recalling arctic skuas.

For me, however, the highlight was a party of a dozen harlequin ducks swimming and feeding amongst the floating kelp offshore, the drakes resplendent in their colourful plumage, a mixture of deep blue, maroon and white. Being sea duck they feed on underwater molluscs, diving for up to 30 seconds, before bobbing back up to the surface like a cork.

So after a week in British Columbia we boarded the Transcanadian train for the 3000-mile journey across Canada to Toronto, during which time the train was to be our home for the next three days.

Stunning views on trip across Canada

October 1999

Canada is the second largest country in the world, and it certainly has some of the longest trains. The one we travelled on from the Pacific to the Atlantic coast comprised 25 carriages, was pulled by three locomotives, and was an incredible half-a-mile long! From the glass dome of the Skyline Car, which was the last carriage on the train, it was an awesome sight to watch it snaking its way through deep river-valleys, alongside mountain lakes and past the magnificent Rockies.

At one point the train slowed as we passed the site of a recent derailment, where grain had spilt from overturned goods wagons. Here a black bear was feasting on this unexpected cache of food. Unfortunately tall firs grew close to the track through the rugged mountainous scenery of the Rockies and very few signs of wildlife were seen. However, once we reached the central plains of Canada, we were treated to a vista of huge prairie lands extending from horizon to horizon.

It's not always easy to identify birds from a fast-moving train and far less so when they are ones on the other side of the world from home. However, there was no mistaking the skein of 200 snow geese, winging their way south in V-formation. The majority were of the dark "blue phase", but there were also some of the "white phase" snow geese, with their contrasting black flight feathers. This would have been one of the many flocks moving south in autumn, into the southern states of North America, to escape the harsh winter of their arctic breeding grounds.

These open prairies, of course, would have originally been covered by the enormous forests that carpeted much of Canada. Now all that remained were secondary woods, consisting largely of aspen, the leaves of which were beginning to turn to their glorious golden autumn hues. Hedgerows were clearly never a feature of the Canadian landscape and fields of ripe sunflowers, extending to over 100 acres each, were commonplace. Herds of cattle wandered the extensive prairies, where at one time bison would have roamed, and at one point a lone coyote was seen stalking near the railway track.

Brief stops to take on fuel and water were made at Jasper, Edmonton and Winnipeg, before we reached the wetlands of Ontario. For nearly a day we travelled across bogs, and past lakes and rivulets, many favoured by wildfowl, which included black duck, blue-winged teal and hooded merganser. And so we arrived at Toronto for the final part of our trip - a week around the Great Lakes.

Welcome return to the Great Lakes

October 1999

For me, the final part of our trip to Canada was a pleasant return to the Great Lakes, an area that I had visited twice before in spring, during the early 1990s.

The Great Lakes, are just that, and standing on the sandy shore it was hard to believe that we were not on a coastal sea shore (Plate 12). On one day, in particular, the strong onshore winds produced waves several feet high, but the ring-billed gulls drinking at the water's edge reminded us that this was indeed fresh and not salt water.

In spring, Point Pelee is one of the most popular places for birders to visit but a trip in autumn is totally different. There were very few other birdwatchers present when we were there last week and it was a joy to be able to seek out and identify the birds ourselves. Perhaps the most spectacular were the loose parties of noisy blue jays, often over 50 strong, flying low over the tree tops towards the southern tip of Point Pelee, from where they would cross the watery expanse to North America.

Of all the birds we saw at Pelee, the northern flicker was surely the gaudiest and most bizarrely marked. It is one of the commonest members of the woodpecker family in North America, and is the size of our green woodpecker. However, the upperparts are brown with black barring contrasting with its white rump, while the buff under-parts are boldly marked with black and the underwings are yellow!

But probably the greatest attraction to European birders are the American warblers. These are small, brightly coloured and highly active birds that behave in much the same way as their European counterparts, although they are in no way related to them. While the numbers in autumn do not match those present in spring, careful searching of the trees and bushes at Pelee can still be very rewarding at this time of year.

On our first morning at Pelee, I was lucky enough to find a fine male Connecticut warbler grubbing around in the low scrub with a couple of white-throated sparrows. This was a bird that I had missed on both my previous trips to Pelee but there was no mistaking its deep purply-blue head and upper breast, and distinct white orbital ring. Another bird, which I was pleased to find early one morning on the tip of Point Pelee, was an American avocet. Similar in general appearance to ours but with a grey head and neck in winter plumage, this bird was a rarity in the Great Lakes and caused much excitement amongst the local birdwatchers. It was almost like being back home!

Recalling the azure waters of Tobago

January 2000

A few months ago, I described some of the highlights of a visit I made to Trinidad in July. During the same trip I also spent three days on its smaller sister island of Tobago. Perhaps some of my recollections from there will help to brighten up an otherwise cold winter's day in England.

The short flight from Trinidad to Tobago takes only about 20 minutes, but the scenery, culture and birdlife of the two islands is quite different. If it's possible, Tobago is even more laid back than Trinidad and being much smaller, the beautiful, deep azure-blue sea is visible from most parts of the island. We stayed at the Blue Waters Inn at Speyside, a charming bay at the north-eastern corner of the island. As elsewhere in the Caribbean, many of the birds are remarkably tame (Plate 12) and meal times are often spent in their company. Bananaquits, small black and yellow birds, are regular visitors to dining areas, where they share your fruit juice, fresh fruits and even sugar from the sugar bowl.

Many of the flowering shrubs in the hotel grounds attract diminutive humming-birds. The males often appear uniformly dark, until the light catches their iridescent plumage at the right angle. Then instantly they become transformed into real gems, none more so than the ruby-topaz hummingbird with its brilliant orange breast.

The national bird of Tobago is the rufous-vented chachalaca. A brown game bird, the size of a small turkey, it has a very loud and persistent call. Groups of them can often be heard calling from the forest around the hotel, particularly at dawn! Incidentally, the name chachalaca is onomatopoeic, as are cuckoo and curlew.

But, for me, the highlight of our trip was a visit to the small offshore island of Little Tobago. Our transport was a glass-bottomed boat that we boarded at the hotel quay. During the short sea crossing we saw many colourful fish around the coral, clearly visible through the glass hull. Little Tobago is uninhabited by man, but is home to a large colony of seabirds. Perhaps, the most attractive are the red-billed tropicbirds, tern-like birds with incredibly long tail streamers, making them so elegant in flight. One pair had nested only a few feet from the path and we were able to photograph the well-grown nestling at arm's length!

Enjoying the rich birdlife of Costa Rica

April 2000

Just over a week ago, I returned from a most enjoyable trip to Costa Rica, organised by Norfolk & Suffolk Wildlife Holidays. When the country was first "discovered" by Christopher Columbus in 1502, many of the natives were wearing gold decorations and so the area became known as *"costa rica"* which translated means "rich coast". But while subsequent events showed that it is not well endowed with natural resources, it certainly is rich in birdlife (Plate 13).

Although one of the smallest of the Central American countries, being only the size of Wales, it possesses a large range of habitats from lowland mangroves and rain forests, to volcanoes and montane forests. As a result of its biodiversity and geographical location, over 800 species of birds have been recorded here, of which we were lucky to be able to see almost 400.

Our trip started on the drier Pacific coast, where we were initially based at La Pacifica, alongside the Rio Corobici. As so often happens abroad, the grounds of our hotel provided an excellent introduction to the birds of this fascinating country, with our first hummingbirds, as well as Costa Rica's national bird, the clay-coloured robin. With so many dazzlingly plumaged birds present, it seemed strange to have chosen a rather drab brown one, recalling our female blackbird, but then it does occur nationwide. La Pacifica is also one of the best known sites for the boat-billed heron, a species of night heron with an extraordinarily broad, boat-shaped bill.

On our second day, we were up at 3.30am, in order to arrive at Palo Verde by dawn. Although not far away, the journey took us nearly two hours, driving along a very bumpy and dusty rough track. As dawn broke we found ourselves in an area of dry scrub, before we arrived at the extensive wetland reserve. Vast stands of cattails (better known as bulrushes in Europe), interspersed with shallow pools, stretched as far as the eye could see.

In front of us a flock of several hundred black-bellied whistling ducks had gathered, accompanied by a few muscovies - genuine wild ones, all black except for a white forewing, unlike the more familiar ones seen on farmyard ponds. Great blue herons, snowy egrets, roseate spoonbills and limpkins paraded around the edges of the pools, while turkey vultures quartered the cattails, recalling marsh harriers in Norfolk. But perhaps best of all, was a fine male peregrine which made several half-hearted passes over the wildfowl, scattering the flock in all directions.

Our quest for the resplendent quetzal

April 2000
Although it's necessary to spend a lot of time travelling in Costa Rica, in order to see a variety of habitats, the journeys are always interesting, none more so than that from the Pacific coast to the Savegre Valley.

As we steadily climbed along the winding mountainous roads, we passed many coffee and sugar cane plantations, while the roadsides were carpeted with many of our familiar garden and household plants, growing wild. Impatiens (perhaps better known as Busy Lizzies) grew in profusion, while begonias and ageratum jostled for space with the taller poinsettias and many varieties of giant fern.

At almost 11,000ft, the road crossed the paramo, a mountain plateau covered with stunted vegetation. This included the only native species of bamboo in Costa Rica, which reaches a maximum height of only two feet, compared with 80ft for the introduced banana bamboo. A brief stop at this high altitude, where anything more than gentle exertion brought on altitude sickness, enabled us to see the volcano junco. This species, related to the sparrows, looks remarkably like a dunnock, as it shuffles around keeping near to the low vegetation.

We were soon driving down into the Savegre Valley, through which passes the Rio Savegre, a beautiful fast-flowing, boulder-strewn river hosting American dipper and a small grey and black flycatcher that lives alongside the water, called the torrent tyrannulet. Two brothers, out on a hunting trip, first discovered this valley in 1952, since when the lodge they built has become a favourite destination for birders visiting the area. Monteverde may be more famous, but the Savegre Valley is considered to be the best place in Costa Rica to see the resplendent quetzal - in fact it was the location for the filming of the species for the BBC's series The Life of Birds.

On our first walk through the montane forest, which covers the steep-sided valley, we were treated to close views of our first male resplendent quetzal - and what a bird it is! About the size of a crow, but vivid green with a bright red belly and white tail, its size accentuated by 2ft-long green tail streamers.

The species nests in trees, and our next encounter with a quetzal was of a male incubating. All that was visible were the two long, slender, pointed tail streamers hanging out of the nesting hole, imitating perfectly the leaves of tree ferns which hung from many of the forest trunks.

Our next stop was to be in the steamy, Caribbean rain forest, with yet more exotic birds to see.

Sight of hanging gold in rain forest

April 2000

The Caribbean and Pacific slopes of Costa Rica play host to two entirely different sets of birds, and so by crossing the central mountain range we were able to find many new birds even during our second week.

Our first stop on the Caribbean side was at Rancho Naturalista, a lodge set in the rain forest of the lower to middle elevations of the Talamanca range. Our days started at 5.30am with coffee on the balcony which overlooked the Rio Tuis Valley. Hummingbird feeders by the balcony attracted many colourful species from the diminutive snowcap to the much larger green-crowned brilliant. Bananas and rice placed on bird tables in the garden below the balcony proved irresistible to scarlet-rumped tanagers, brown jays and the noisy Montezuma oropendolas (Plate 13). These crow-sized birds with long yellow tails enthralled us with their bizarre swinging displays from which they get their name, which translated literally means "hanging gold".

Each day we explored the narrow forest trails which steadily wound their way up the hillsides and each day brought us new excitements. Although we might walk for some time without actually seeing any birds, we were often aware of their presence from the strange calls coming from deep within the humid forest. Our excellent local guide, Freddy Madrigal, also warned us always to be on the look out for snakes and not to venture off the narrow trail. One small boa constrictor was found entwined around a branch at head level, from where it obligingly posed for photographs, while another species, a parrot snake, was being mobbed by a barred woodcreeper whose nest it had just robbed.

Troops of mantled howler monkeys were always a delight to watch, as they moved and fed in the canopy high above us, and they certainly lived up to their name at night! But perhaps the most amusing was a Central American spider monkey that gave us a fine performance of swinging between trees and vines, using its extraordinary long, spider-like limbs and tail.

The trees were also home to two and three-toed sloths, a four-foot long member of the weasel family called a tayra and several species of squirrels; while amongst the ground-feeding mammals that we were lucky enough to see were coatimundi, collared peccary and best of all, a collared anteater.

Our final few days were spent in the Caribbean foothills at Selva Verde, where brightly coloured parrots, toucans, trogons and manakins provided a fitting climax to a memorable holiday.

County Cork's mosaic of colour

September 2000

One of my favourite Irish folk songs is The Fields of Athenry. Judging by the number of times Fran and I heard it during a week in Ireland, earlier this month, it is also very popular with the residents of the Emerald Isle.

As we drove west from Cork, it was a delight to pass along winding roads, largely free of traffic, through a mosaic of small, irregularly-shaped meadows bordered by tall, unkempt hedgerows. Many fields contained surprisingly large herds of black and white Friesians, at a stocking rate far higher than occurs in East Anglia. Presumably the higher annual rainfall results in far lusher vegetation, which in turn supports more head of cattle.

Every farm that we passed hosted swallows, many perched like sentinels on the roadside wires. Whatever has caused the number of swallows here at home to fall certainly does not appear to have effected the Irish population. However, as in the rest of the British Isles, rooks were abundant, as were magpies; while carrion crows were replaced by the handsome grey and black, hooded crows.

The further west we travelled, the more rugged became the scenery and we soon found ourselves skirting the many small, rocky inlets fashioned by the mighty Atlantic. The narrow roads were lined by thick fuchsia hedges, so characteristic of this part of Ireland, while the orange spikes of montbretia added colour to the verges. The surrounding low moorland was a beautiful patchwork of purple and golden-yellow, where heathers and dwarf gorse grew in profusion.

At last we arrived at our destination of Baltimore, a sleepy, quaint, if rather run-down, fishing village, nestling on the side of Roaring Water Bay. Like other villages in this part of Cork, the grey rendering of many of the houses had been painted in bright azure blue, magenta, buttercup yellow or some other vivid hue. Although this would have been totally out of place in a busy town, down here it seemed perfectly natural!

One of the best walks in this area was to the hilltop above Lough Ine, the steep path passing through some beautiful woodland. A dense coating of moss and lichens covered the trunks and branches of the sessile oaks, and there was a thick carpet of creeping ivy over the slopes either side of the path, interspersed with clumps of taller ferns. The view from the top was magnificent, well worth the effort of the climb, and from there we were able to see across to Cape Clear, our destination for the morrow.

Returning to Cape Clear was unwise

September 2000

For me, the trip to western Ireland with Fran in early September, would have been incomplete without visiting the island of Cape Clear that I had visited last in 1967. As we stood on the small quay at Baltimore, waiting to board the ferry for the short sea crossing, I wondered what changes would be apparent after an interval of 33 years! Perhaps it would have been wiser not to have risked tarnishing cherished memories from my earlier birdwatching days? Only time would tell.

The small open boat that I remember making my earlier crossing in had been replaced by a larger vessel, onto the deck of which supplies for the islanders were being loaded. At least she was still named *Naomh Ciaran*, meaning St Kieran, the patron saint of Cape Clear.

Once aboard, we were soon passing the myriad of small islands that lay off the mainland and in less than an hour we were moored in the safety of Cape Clear's North Harbour. I was immediately struck by a collection of ramshackle old cars that were lined up on the quayside. Here was the first major change. Back in 1967, cars were absent from the island, transport being provided by the odd tractor and trailer! Nowadays, apparently, there is no restriction and any clapped out old banger, which is no longer considered road worthy on the mainland, is considered suitable for Cape Clear! Unfortunately, when they do eventually give up the ghost, they are simply dumped in the nearest field.

I was keen to show Fran the rugged, Atlantic-facing south-western points of the island and so we headed off along the uneven track leading to Blananarragaun. Stonechats were in evidence along many of the dry stone walls, while occasional robins sought shelter in the bracken. It was at about this point that I noticed the second major change on the island - the presence of notices warning about bulls and advising would-be walkers to "keep out". On my last visit we were free to wander at will. It soon became apparent that we would not be able to reach the south-western part of the island. However, we were far enough over to be able to see the gaunt outline of the Fastnet lighthouse, perched on top of its isolated rock - the most southerly point of Ireland.

As we turned back, we could hear in the distance the characteristic calls of choughs, but unfortunately were unable to locate them. Perhaps, it had been unwise to return after all.

Mizen Head the setting for our perfect day

September 2000
The west coast of Ireland is renowned for the large number of seabirds that annually pass offshore. As I described in yesterday's column, Fran and I were thwarted in our attempt to witness this passage at first hand, during our day trip to the island of Cape Clear. So the following day found us driving around Roaring Water Bay towards Mizen Head, one of the many rocky headlands which jut out into the wild waters of the Atlantic around the south-west tip of mainland Ireland.

We made a brief stop at a muddy estuary near Crookhaven where a fine selection of waders included a scattering of black-tailed godwits, the vanguard of the many thousand that overwinter in southern Ireland. Our attention was attracted by a guttural barking overhead and on looking up we watched a pair of ravens lazily flying across the bay - the largest member of the crow family with the massive bill, so obvious in flight.

The road began to climb and we were soon perched on a grassy slope by Mizen Head (Plate 14) with Atlantic rollers crashing on the rocks several hundred feet below us. With the sun peaking out from behind some cotton wool clouds and the azure-blue sea extending as far as the eye could see, it was the perfect setting for a relaxing day.

For the next three hours, a constant stream of seabirds passed offshore. Black and white gannets in straggly lines, orderly chevrons or just loose groups were always in view, with the occasional birds making spectacular dives into the water after fish. Thousands of Manx shearwaters flew west in scattered parties of up to 100, the apparently black upperparts seeming to change to dark chocolate brown when the sun appeared, each bird skimming the surface of the sea, faithfully following the waves and troughs. A few of the larger and all dark, sooty shearwaters, were with the Manx, while further variety was provided by a pomarine skua harrying some Sandwich terns.

The steep cliffs here were also home to several pairs of choughs and it was a delight to watch these jackdaw-sized, all black crows probing the short grass sward with their bright red, decurved bills. They clearly revelled in the updraughts above the cliffs, as they wheeled around in pairs, side slipping and twisting this way and that; their bonds renewed by gentle pecking at each other's necks as they landed on the precipitous cliff face, where their bright red legs and bills contrasted beautifully with the grey granite.

This was truly the Ireland that I remembered and loved.

Ecuador is a land of great contrasts

November 2000

Last week I returned from my first visit to South America, a two-week trip with Naturetrek to Ecuador, a country named after its position on the equator. Although small, Ecuador is a land of great contrasts. One day we were in a steamy Amazonian rain forest (Plate 14) and the next on a cold and bleak Andean mountain top at over 14,000ft.

After flying into Quito, the country's capital, which itself is situated at 9,000ft, we spent a couple of days acclimatizing, before making for the higher passes. The scenery here was majestic. Surrounded, as we were, by towering cloud forest-covered mountains, as far as the eye could see.

On one memorable morning we rose before dawn to watch the sun rise from behind the snow covered peak of the volcano Antisana. At over 17,000ft it is one of the highest points in Ecuador and the sight of the sun reflecting off the deep snow is a memory I shall forever cherish.

The bird life was rich and varied with different species appearing as we climbed higher and higher. Perhaps the most striking were the brilliantly coloured mountain--tanagers, their names describing well their beautiful appearance, such as the scarlet-bellied and the blue-winged mountain-tanagers.

We crossed many fast-flowing torrents, the water cutting through deep mountain gorges eventually to feed the mighty Amazon. One bird that we all wanted to see was the torrent duck, a species that has adapted to these raging mountain rivers. Incredibly, our sharp-eyed local guide Pancho spotted one on a riverside rock several hundred feet below the road on which we were travelling. It was a fine drake with brown upperparts, and a black and white striped head. Through the telescope we were able to appreciate the skill of this superbly adapted bird as it expertly dived into the fast flowing turbulent water, to reappear 20 seconds later as it climbed out on to another boulder.

Travelling ever higher we came to the desolate and inhospitable paramo, an area lying above the tree line. Here all the vegetation is stunted and few birds are to be found. We were very fortunate to locate a pair of the much sought-after rufous-bel-lied seedsnipe feeding nearby amongst the tussocks. Despite behaving and looking very much like grouse, seedsnipe are placed in a family of their own.

Although we failed to see an Andean condor we left this part of Ecuador more than happy with the long list of birds that we had encountered.

Amazonian rain forests are full of marvels

November 2000
As I explained in yesterday's column, I've just returned from Ecuador where the second half of our trip took us into the Amazonian basin. The tropical rain forests of the Amazon cover an amazing 2.5 million sq miles that are inhabited by an awe inspiring variety of birds, plants, insects and mammals.

Our base was to be Sacha Lodge, a 5,000-acre reserve where our English tour leader for Naturetrek, Andy Tucker, had worked for a year previously. After a short flight over the Andes from Quito, we landed at the town of Puerto Francisco de Orellano, named after the Spanish lieutenant-general who is accredited with discovering the Amazon.

From here we boarded a motorised canoe for the 50-mile trip along the River Napo, the major tributary of the River Amazon. We were soon spotting the typical birds of this riverine habitat, such as black caracara, yellow-billed and large-billed terns, as well as ospreys and spotted sandpipers, both winter visitors from North America.

On arrival at the reserve we still had to cross Pilchicocha Lake by dugout canoe to reach Sacha Lodge (Plate 15). What a setting! Buildings constructed solely from local materials, surrounded on all sides by dense tropical rain forest and the beautiful Pilchicocha Lake, home to caimans (members of the alligator family), electric eels and piranhas, which we were assured were vegetarian!

One of the highlights of a stay at Sacha is a morning spent in the treetop hide, which stands 140ft high and is built around a giant kapok tree. From the viewing platform a unique insight into the bird life of the canopy is possible (Plate 16). A constant stream of brightly-coloured tanagers flitted from tree to tree, including some really special ones such as paradise, masked crimson and golden tanagers to name but three species. A pair of cream-coloured woodpeckers was particularly beautiful while the white-throated toucans displayed a stunning mixture of colours. The haunting cries of a pair of laughing falcons, with red howler monkeys calling in the distance, made for an unforgettable experience.

Back at the lake, we searched for another speciality of the lowland waterways of the northern Neotropics, the hoatzin. We soon located two clambering through the waterside vegetation. Over two feet in length and with a long, shaggy crest, they really were some of the most bizarre-looking birds that I have ever seen.

Tomorrow I shall describe the thrill of visiting a parrot-lick where the birds gather to obtain clay, which is thought to counteract toxins ingested in unripe fruit.

Parrots gather for their vital dose of clay

November 2000

During my recent visit to Ecuador, 12 species of parrots were recorded, ranging in size from the small, cobalt-winged parakeet to the large and striking, blue and yellow macaw. Macaws are one of the largest members of the parrot family, their size accentuated by very long pointed tails. They are almost invariably seen in pairs, either as they fly over the canopy or as they acrobatically display and feed amongst the tree-top branches.

Parrots are vegetarian with most species taking a wide variety of seeds, fruits, nuts and leaves, their powerful, curved bills having evolved to enable them to obtain the highly nutritional content of hard seeds. Unfortunately, eating or simply cutting through unripe, tannin-rich pulp, or consuming certain seeds, exposes the birds to distasteful or even toxic alkaloid substances. Many species of parrots visit so-called clay-licks, where they scrape off and eat particles of clay. It's believed that the clay helps to counteract these potential poisons.

On one of the mornings of our stay at Sacha Lodge we were taken by motorised canoe along the River Napo to witness the unforgettable spectacle of hundreds of parrots gathering at one of these traditional clay-licks. The tops of the palms and cecropias were crowded with hundreds of noisy, squawking parrots, preparing to drop down to the vertical bank of clay. Four species were present, including the aptly-named blue-headed parrot and the larger all green, mealy parrot. Some of the alkaloids ingested by the parrots, when feeding on unripe fruits, are stimulants. Researchers have noticed that macaws often arrive at the clay-licks in a very excited state, but appear considerably calmer after sampling the clay!

After four marvellous days at Sacha Lodge, we reluctantly returned to Quito, for our last couple of days in Ecuador. There was still one species that we were all hoping to see and our leader, Andy Tucker, knew of a site where, with luck, we should be able to see a gathering of males displaying at a so-called "lek".

So despite the only poor weather of the trip, we once more drove up into the Andes amid increasingly overcast skies and thickening mist. For two hours we drove along a narrow and tortuous mountain road, before arriving at an extensive area of cloud forest. Here we witnessed one of the greatest spectacles of the bird world - the communal display of the Andean cock-of-the-rock. Bright, scarlet coloured birds, the size of jackdaws but with large, permanently erected crests, postured or flew from tree to tree, while calling loudly.

This truly was a fitting climax to a superb holiday in Ecuador.

Novel look at the island of Cephallonia

May 2001

The only time that I ever seem to read a novel is while sitting on a beach on holiday, and it was while enjoying a relaxing week in St Lucia two years ago that I read Louis de Bernieres' highly-acclaimed book, Captain Corelli's Mandolin. It brought back happy memories of our first family holiday to a Greek island in 1988, when we visited the delightful island of Cephallonia, in which the novel is set.

Following the premiere of the film Captain Corelli's Mandolin, it now seems impossible to open a paper without finding an article about Cephallonia, but so far I have not seen one extolling the delights of the island's natural history. That is until now!

Cephallonia is the largest and most mountainous of the Ionian Islands, its tallest peak, Megalos Soros, reaching over 1600 metres. Much of the central hilly part of the island is covered by a native species of pine, although unfortunately vast swathes had been destroyed by forest fires the year before our visit. I'm sure that by now this will have recovered fully.

One of the commonest birds throughout the island was the woodchat shrike, usually seen perched on the roadside wires. The foothills of the mountains were home to tawny pipits, the large rather plain pipits, so characteristic of southern Europe, that strut around like wagtails. While flying around the higher slopes were ravens and buzzards, whose paths were often crossed by dashing alpine swifts. The scrubby areas and olive groves hosted both Sardinian and subalpine warblers, as well as the occasional more drably plumaged olivaceous warbler.

However, it wasn't only birds that caught my attention, we were there in July and butterflies were present in abundance. Clouded yellows, scarce swallowtails, southern white admirals and eastern rock graylings were widespread. But my greatest thrill came from finding a two-tailed pasha, a large dark brown butterfly with two "tails" on the hind-wing and a rich mix of colours and patterns on the underside of each wing.

A narrow, mountain stream near the village of Ayios Nicolaos proved particularly rewarding for dragonflies, and it was here that I saw my first ever beautiful demoiselle, and how it lived up to its name - the male with its most exquisite deep blue wings.

Of the ten species of dragonfly that I identified on Cephallonia, only two had previously been recorded on the island. Clearly it had not been visited before by a dragonfly enthusiast! I'm sure that there must still be much to discover, but you'd better get there soon!